ESSAYS ON
NEIL M. GUNN

Edited by David Morrison

Printed & Published by John Humphries,
at Caithness Books, Thurso, Caithness, Scotland.

CONTENTS

NOTES ON CONTRIBUTORS

<u>David Morrison</u>. Deputy County Librarian of Caithness. Well known as a poet, having published four volumes to date. Since January 1970 he has been editing "Scotia", a monthly broadsheet on Scottish Life and Literature. A Glaswegian by birth, he has lived in Caithness for four years.

<u>John L. Broom</u>. A graduate of Edinburgh University and then Oxford, he was ordained a minister of the Unitarian Church in 1948. Subsequently he entered the library profession and is at present Local History, Music and Fine Art Librarian for the County of Aberdeen. He has contributed many articles to a variety of magazines and writes a monthly column for "Scotia". He has completed a biography of the Scottish Socialist leader, John Maclean, (as yet unpublished), and is currently working on a Critical Companion to Twentieth Century Scottish Fiction.

<u>Francis Thompson</u>. A lecturer at Inverness Technical College, he has written books on "Harris and Lewis", "St. Kilda and other Hebridean outliers", and has contributed articles to a variety of papers and magazines. The Managing Director of Club Leabhar (Highland Book Club), he is also well known in Gaelic circles as founder member of An Cruinne, the editor of the "Celtic League Annual" and ex-editor of "Sruth".

<u>Francis Russell Hart</u>. Professor of English at the University of Virginia. A New Englander by birth and education, he became an enthusiastic reader of Neil Gunn during a post-graduate Fulbright Year (1955-6) in Edinburgh. He has been engaged for the past five years on a book about the novel in Scotland and a biographical study of Neil Gunn.

<u>J.B. Caird</u>. H.M.I. for Ross and Cromarty, formerly Sutherland, Caithness and Orkney, he graduated in English under Sir Herbert Grierson. His lifelong interest in Scottish literature, both Lowland and Gaelic, dates from the time when, as a student, he first met Hugh MacDiarmid and Sorley Maclean. He lectures extensively on Scottish Literature.

<u>W.R. Aitken</u>. Senior Lecturer in Bibliographical Studies, University of Strathclyde, his "History of the Public Library Movement in Scotland to 1955" was published this year. His "Hugh MacDiarmid, a Chronological Bibliography" has proved to be essential to researchers and over the years he has done a great deal of work for Scottish literature in the bibliographical sphere.

INTRODUCTION

On the 8th November Neil M. Gunn celebrates his eightieth birthday and this book of essays, published in the county of his birth, pays tribute to a novelist who has achieved much of lasting significance. I agree with John L. Broom in his essay when he states that Gunn is "in the very front rank in the field of 20th Century Scottish fiction." Kurt Wittig in his excellent book, "The Scottish Tradition in Literature", (Oliver and Boyd, 1958) sang Gunn's praises by saying, "It seems to me, however, that modern Scottish fiction reaches its highest peak in the novels of NEIL M. GUNN (1891), so far the only Scottish novelist whose work in some measure embodies all the ideals of the Scots Renaissance."

In his book The Key to the Chest, Gunn has said,

"Man must for ever move, like a liberator, through
his own unconsciousness."

The author cannot see Man as living in a vacuum present but as being a part of a great linked chain. Wittig gets it exactly right when he says,

"He is not interested in chance happenings; he is looking
for the pattern of life, the underlying ritual, the myth."

Although Gunn has achieved a great deal in his recording and interpreting Highland life, my consuming interest with his work is his symbolism and mysticism which at times can be extremely complex. To read Gunn is to exercise your own mind in a manner which demands much self-analysis.

In our great, sprawling urban societies there is not much room or time for contemplation and as we grow more and more materialistic in outlook, our faculties, which should be exercised in self-revelation, are quickly becoming dulled.

Concerned as I am with the quality of life, and very much concerned about the future, Gunn's books are now constant companions of mine, and I find that I can become greatly angered when someone suggests that he is an escapist or that he wrote of a way of life which has almost gone now. Time marches on, ways of life change, but the great quality of Gunn is that he is concerned with the spiritual qualities of Man. This surely must concern all thinking men of any time or any place.

I am confident that as the years go by a great deal more critical attention will be paid to Gunn, and it is a healthy sign that some of his works are now prescribed texts in educational establishments. In the final analysis what is really important is not academic treatises but that Gunn should be read by a wide audience in successive generations.

I am also confident that the essays in this book will whet the appetite of those who do not already know Gunn's works or those who know only a few novels. It is essential to read the whole range of this novelist to come to a deep understanding of the man, and if the effort is made, a lasting experience will result. Many of us have the urgent need to trace the rivers of our minds to the source. The important thing is not what we find at the source but what we see and learn on our way.

I must thank the authors of these essays for being so willing to pay tribute to Gunn; the Scottish Arts Council and Caithness County Council for financial assistance in publishing the book, A.M.E. Luciani for the splendid photograph and Barbara Myatt for the cover drawing and illustrations. Finally I must thank Neil M. Gunn for a lifetime's work.

David Morrison, Reaster, 1971.

NEIL M. GUNN

BIOGRAPHICAL NOTES

Neil Miller Gunn was born in Dunbeath in Caithness on 8th November, 1891, the sixth child of a family of nine. The fishing village of his birth and early environment was obviously to play a great part in the development of later years. It is interesting to note that most of the crew that his father employed for his few boats were from the West and Gaelic speakers. When he was eleven he went to live in Galloway and by his mid-teens was in London working in the Civil Service. He started in London in 1906, and later in his life as an officer of Customs and Excise he travelled all over Scotland. His work brought him in contact with the people of many communities and obviously this gave him a deep insight into ways of life and thought. We can attribute Second Sight to his life in the West. He was a regular contributor to many magazines, such as "The Scots Magazine", "Chamber's Journal", "The Cornhill", "The Northern Review", "The Saltire Review" and the "Scottish Nation". His first novel, The Grey Coast, was published in 1926. His sixth novel, Highland River, won for him the Tait Black Memorial Prize for 1937.

Although Gunn is to be regarded as a novelist, he has also written plays; in the "Voice of Scotland Series" there appears his Whisky and Scotland which has that beautiful sub-title, "A Practical and Spiritual Survey"; a travel book Off in a Boat which also shows his ingenuity in expanding on a title - It is written "For the crew (his wife), this simple record of a holiday in a boat, bought in ignorance and navigated by faith and a defective engine". Then there is his last work, an autobiography with a difference The Atom of Delight.

In the life of Gunn it can definitely be stated that he has been fortunate in the fact that his employment brought him into close contact with almost every community in Scotland. The artistry of the man is clearly shown in the manner in which he has been able to assimilate so much of the pulse of communities into his writing. He now lives in Kessock, in a house which has a commanding view of the Firth and Inverness.

THE NOVELS OF NEIL M GUNN

John L. Broom

Though Neil Gunn's novels have received considerable critical acclaim, he has never been a "best-selling" writer, except perhaps in his native Caithness. This popular neglect has probably been due chiefly to the obscurity and allusiveness of his style, and to the symbolical and mystical elements in his work which gradually became more complex as his vision deepened.

The plot of his first novel The Grey Coast (1926) is, however, conventional enough. It tells of the stormy love-affair between Ivor Cormack and Maggie Tait and its attempted frustration by Maggie's crafty Uncle Jeems and Ivor's rival for Maggie's hand, the wicked Dan Tullach. Tullach is rather a stage villian whose "teeth grind, whose eyes gleam like a stoat's and whose face grins in horrible contortions" at one stage of the narrative. Eventually Uncle Jeems dies, and Tullach's nefarious schemes to seduce Maggie are brought to naught by the righteous Ivor. In spite of such crude melodrama, there are some wonderfully evocative and sensitive passages which, to perceptive critics of the time, (e.g. Hugh MacDiarmid in "Contemporary Scottish Studies") marked Gunn out as a new writer of quite exceptional promise. The sea, with which Gunn has such a strong love-hate relationship, dominates the story. "The sea . . . breeds a clear-eyed self-reliance, a silence, a grim courage, which has its reaction in an open-handedness which, not infrequently, slips into a spendthrift recklessness." One of the best scenes describes a poaching expedition with which activity Gunn obviously sympathises, and of which, as he explains in his fascinating autobiography An Atom of Delight (1956), he had personal knowledge. A distinct sense of timelessness pervades the novel, which is set in no particular period. It was published in the same year as Hugh MacDiarmid's "A Drunk Man Looks at the Thistle", and when, at one point, Ivor partakes too freely of alcohol, his reflections bear a curious resemblance to those of MacDiarmid's immortal imbiber.

Gunn's next novel Morning Tide did not appear until 1931. This is a sensitively-told psychological study of boyhood and adolescence. Most of the events are seen through the eyes of young Hugh McBeth who lives with his parents, his sisters Kirsty and Grace, and his brother Alan in a fishing village on the north-east Scottish coast, easily identifiable with Gunn's own birthplace, Dunbeath. Hugh's poaching and fishing expeditions are recounted with much knowledgeable attention to detail, and his dawning sexual awareness is delicately sketched. Watching a girl removing a stain from her dress one day at school he reflects that "the way she spat was entirely feminine, and a small bead of saliva dropped on her breast."

The sea again plays a dominating role in this novel. Hugh's father is a skipper, and his mother both hates and fears the sea. She hates it because it is a rival for her husband's affection, and she fears it because it may one day take him from her. There is a wonderful description of a storm at sea, and a very moving account of Mrs. McBeth's almost fatal illness. Gunn's belief that reality is fundamentally inexpressible appears more than once in the narrative. "Truth is not of words but of vision. Thus many things that are spoken contradict one another, but in the vision there is no contradiction." Though Morning Tide has a rather contrived happy ending, it is on the whole free from the sentimentality which flaws some of Gunn's later works.

Sun Circle (1933) is set in Caithness in the 9th Century A.D., and the theme is the conflict between the old pagan religions of the Picts and Northmen, and Christianity. Aniel, the son of Taran the Bard, is loved by two women, Breeta and Nessa. Nessa is the beautiful daughter of the Christian chief of the tribe Durst and his wife Silas. But Aniel is a pagan, a disciple of the strange Master who conducts mysterious rituals in the woods by night, and Breeta has guilt feelings over her love for him. Yet she is not certain if she herself believes in Christianity.

The marauding Northmen arrive, and in the ensuing battles, both Durst and Taran are killed, and Silas commits suicide. In spite of the fact that he killed her father, the wayward Nessa falls passionately in love with the leader of the invaders, the handsome young Haakon. But his friend, the aged Viking Sweyn, offers cautionary counsel. "There may always be some final man or king to whom you may have to submit, but never submit to any woman . . . The power of a woman can be a more terrible thing than the power of any man because it is a jealous power over his spirit . . . it can move him on to deeds that he is ashamed of before men, to secret black acts that destroy him." Haakon, however, ignores this sage advice, and he and Nessa become lovers. But they are caught in the act by Aniel and his fellow Picts and taken captive. Nessa, trading on Aniel's old love for her, tries to persuade him to betray his comrades. Aniel, overcome by her passion and desirability, at first agrees, but later sees it is impossible. "The Northmen had killed her father, half the tribe, women and children, and she was cleaving to him. What sort of a woman was she? . . . And yet now that he was free of her she was with him more than ever."

Finally, Nessa and Haakon are killed by the Picts, Aniel's mysterious Master dies and he, "delivered to freedom", returns to Breeta.

Although the ending clearly symbolises the historical triumph of Christianity over the pagan religions, this does not necessarily mean that Gunn believes that the former is superior to the latter. As the dying Master reflects: "Aniel would bring back the young chief with his Christian religion . . . But if Aniel had to satisfy his own people in the old ways, then he would do so, even if he had to do it secretly. For there was only one law in the end: the spirit had to be satisfied. In the fulness of time, the Christian religion might satisfy it for it, too, was based on blood and sacrifice. . . our past is in the earth, and our roots are in the past. . . the earth beneath, the sun above, and we, the children of their union. That is all we know, and perhaps all we need to know to find the power that has serenity at its heart."

Sun Circle is an impressive novel of great beauty of style and profundity of thought. But although in essence the story is an absorbing one, it is continually being interrupted to permit of lengthy incursions into Gunn's peculiar world of nature mysticism. As a result the novel has had only a limited appeal.

Butcher's Broom (1934) is probably the most famous of the fictional accounts of the Highland Clearances, although, in my opinion it lacks the emotional impact of both Fionn MacColla's "And the Cock Crew", and Iain Crichton Smith's "Consider the Lilies". In fact, most of the action in Butcher's Broom takes place before the period of the Clearances themselves, and describes the daily life of the Highlanders in the doomed Kildonan village in minute and, at times, tedious detail. The style, as usual, is admirable, with a rich vocabulary and many passages of flowing beauty. With a few deft strokes, Gunn evokes the atmosphere of a social evening in a primitive Highland cottage: "In the centre of this gloom was the fire, and sitting round it their knees drawn together, their heads stooped were the old women like fate, the young women like love, and the small boy with the swallow of life in his hand." His images too are remarkable and original: "As Elie entered Angus Sutherland's house, life met her in a bright tumbling wave." He notes lovingly the enchanting turns of phrase of the Gaelic tongue: "A man or woman might say in greeting, It's the fine day that's in it', as though he were setting the day in the hollow of the world so that they might, with conscious detachment, regard it . . . In truth, it is an immensely old tongue and a thousand years before Mairi, it was richer in its knowledge wider in its range and was given to metaphysics and affairs of state . . . for love-making it is a subtle tongue."

Some of the characters are presented with power and insight. Mairi, "the witch with healing powers who made everything natural", Elie the servant, a girl of spirit, Colin her swain, Murdoch the cripple and Seumas Og, the visionary. A strong sense of the supernatural broods over the novel. Yet, in spite of all the individual felicities, <u>Butcher's Broom</u> as a whole fails to impress. The sad story is told so obliquely and in parts obscurely, that interest in the fate of the folk of Kildonan evaporates before the tragedy of the Clearances finally overtakes them.

<u>Highland River</u> (1937) is, like <u>Morning Tide</u>, a highly personal novel in which Gunn identifies himself with the sensitive young boy Kenn and his rise to manhood in a Caithness village. As with Hugh McBeth, we follow Kenn when he goes poaching and hunting and in his wanderings over the moors, by rivers and the sea. Kenn's father, like Hugh's, is a seaman, a bearded religious patriach and a fanatical Sabbatarian. But his mother has a deeper vision - when Kenn's father suspects (rightly) that his son has been out poaching rabbits on the Sabbath, his mother protects him "And in that moment of time Kenn knew . . . that when the rabbit was produced she would accept it. And there and then was born in him a deep understanding of his mother, of something in her that transcended the religious observances in which she believed, that was bigger than place or time because it recognised the inexorable nature of the needs of daily life."

Unfortunately, Gunn does not tell his story in a straightforward manner, but keeps jumping from Kenn as a boy to Kenn as an adult and back again. The reason for this technique is no doubt to indicate the illusory nature of time, but it has the effect of halting the saga of Kenn just when the reader is becoming really interested in it. The tale is heavy with symbolism. Kenn's desire to trace the river to its source portrays not only his desire to uncover the springs of his own being, but the river itself typifies the history of the race and its source man's state of primeval innocence. Gunn's belief in a remote Golden Age of glorious uncorrupted hunters (which he returns to in <u>Second Sight</u> as we shall see) is very similar to the Diffusionist theory of anthropology, so brilliantly expounded in many of his novels by Lewis Grassic Gibbon.

<u>Highland River</u> contains some of Gunn's most beautiful and evocative poetic prose. It is doubtful if the Caithness landscape will ever again be more lovingly and marvellously delineated than in this novel: "This bare, green, austere Caithness treeless, windswept, rock-bound, hammered by the sea, hammered too by successive races of men, broch builders and sea rovers, Pict and Viking. Against the light Kenn veils his eyes and, wheeling round, sees the Orkneys anchored in the blue sea with the watermark of white on their bows. Brave islands, he feels like saluting them with a shout.

"Westward yet, and the granite peaks of Ben Laoghal, the magic mountain, beckons towards Cape Wrath and the Arctic. Westward still, and all the dark mountains of Sutherland march on Ben More Assynt, beyond which is the Atlantic and the isles of the West."

In Wild Geese Overhead (1939), Gunn temporarily deserted the land and the sea for a novel about city life. The theme is the gradual conversion of a hard-bitten cynical Glasgow journalist, Will Montgomery, into a human being. The not uncommon charge that Gunn is an escapist writer in the romantic Celtic-twilight tradition, is effectively refuted by the uncompromising realism of many of the episodes in this book. Take, for example, the following passage describing Will's experience in the noisome lavatory of the Glasgow pub: "Men's backs and shoulders; one or two swaying in their drink. The fellow next to him was leaning forward, supported by the forehead which pressed against the flagstone wall. All at once, the horizontal pipe a few inches above the man's head noisily gushed out water through its small perforations. The water descended upon his cap, soaked it, and trickled down his face. His whole body convulsed, and his mouth ejected a violent gush of vomit, which hit the flagstone, and spat back upon Will's clothes. Will let out a harsh grunt of disgust, and began wildly brushing the stuff off with his naked hand. Slowly the face twisted round at him. Black burning eyes. The eyes held him, torture drawn to fine points. The face drew back from the wall slowly and steadied, concentrating on Will in a demoniacal satire and hatred. Only as the body squared up did Will notice that the right arm was missing."

There are many individual excellences in Wild Geese Overhead, not least being the delicate compassionate account of Will's strange, asexual friendship with a young prostitute from the slums. But it is too long and overburdened with political discussions which seem to lead nowhere. As Gunn himself wrote of one of them: "It was a long argument . . . intricate in design, full of doubtings and twistings", which is a not inaccurate description of the author's own convoluted manner of expression in this novel. Will's interior monologues, too, seem rather more suited to a book of literary criticism than to a work of fiction. But rarely has the degradation of life in the Glasgow slums during the Depression and the contrast between such horrors and the useless comfortable existence of the idle rich as represented by some of Will's well-off friends, been so graphically portrayed. Finally, Will, after undergoing much mental and physical suffering, achieves self-liberation and fulfilment, symbolised by the "wild geese overhead".

The action of Second Sight (1940), takes place in a Highland shooting lodge during one summer. The quarry is deer, particularly a great sta

known as King Brude. One day, Alick MacDonald, stalker to Harry
Kingsley, one of the guests at the lodge, has a vision of four men carry
ing a dead body. When pressed, he confesses that the men are Sir John
Marway, owner of the lodge, George his nephew, Angus, another stalke
and Maclean, the head gamekeeper. The identity of the corpse he refus
es to reveal, but Harry suspects it is Geoffrey Smith, another guest an
a confirmed materialist and sceptic. Geoffrey is determined to be the
slayer of King Brude, and one day when he is out hunting the elusive an
mal, a sudden mist descends . . .

Gunn is a firm believer in the supernatural (in Butcher's Broom indeed, he suggests that second sight may be possessed by some animals
as well as men) and in this novel there is much interesting discussion
of the possibility of precognition and of J. W. Dunne's theory of serial-
ism and the Fourth Dimension. The remarkable prophecies of the
Brahan Seer, the celebrated 17th Century Highland mystic, are also
investigated. One of the most intriguing questions raised is: Can we,
by the exercise of our free will prevent an event "foreseen" by second
sight from taking place? If Geoffrey and George can be persuaded to
leave the lodge and never return together, surely Alick's prevision
cannot possibly come to pass? A sub-plot in the book is the developing
but rather novelettish love-affair between Harry Kingsley and Sir John
Marway's daughter, Helen.

For those interested in psychical research this a must. The suspens
as to whether Alick's prophecy of doom will in fact be fulfilled, is well
sustained, and the denouement is ingeniously contrived. The morality
stag-hunting is not questioned, though certain rules of fair play should
be observed (e.g. the deer should never be driven towards the stalkers
At one point Helen does feel momentary sympathy for a harried deer,
but immediately she decides that this is like "a betrayal of Harry, of al
her men, the hunting men, the hunters that came over the horizon after
primeval horizon, through dark ages and medieval ages, into the Sept-
ember sun of this day she was alive in."

The title of The Silver Darlings (1941) refers to "the lithe silver fish,
the swift flashing ones, hundreds and thousands of them . . . the silver
darlings". It is a long, rambling story set in Sutherland and Caithness
during the first half of the 19th Century. After Tormad has been press
ganged into the Navy while out fishing near Helmsdale his pregnant wife
Catrine, journeys to Dunster (Gunn's native Dunbeath again) to stay wit
a friend of her mother's, Kirsty Mackay. Nearing her destination, she
meets Skipper Roddy Sinclair who finds himself greatly attracted to the
spirited girl. Catrine is received well by the hospitable Kirsty and decides to have her baby and make her home there, as she is convinced
that Tormad will never return.

The rest of the novel is mainly concerned with the relationship between Catrine and Roddy, and the emotional and spiritual development of Catrine's son, Finn. The portrait of Finn as a young boy is drawn with sensitivity and insight, recalling the similar evocations of childhood in The Grey Coast, Morning Tide and Highland River. There is a stunningly beautiful description of Finn's pursuit and killing of a butterfly (in the Gaelic, "God's fool") and subsequent remorse and guilt. "Already", writes Gunn, "the terrible knowledge of good and evil was in him." Other memorable scenes include a graphic account of the cholera epidemic of 1832, a realistic description of a revivalist meeting in Lewis, and, above all, a wonderful piece of narrative writing recounting Finn's ascent of a dangerous precipice in search of food and water when Roddy's boat is forced to take shelter off the summer isles following a terrible storm at sea.

In The Silver Darlings, we find the same hostility between the land and the sea as in Morning Tide. The sea is the destroyer, whereas the earth is the giver of life. Traditionally, the bountiful land is identified with the feminine principle, and so the women in both novels both hate and fear the murdering sea. However, in spite of press-gangs, storm and plague, The Silver Darlings is basically an optimistic novel, depicting the Scottish fishing industry in its palmiest days. The story is told in a much more straightforward fashion than is usual with Gunn and is none the worse for that. Though the ending is rather over-sentimentalised, this novel must be reckoned one of Gunn's finest achievements.

Gunn's next full-length novel was The Serpent (1943) which was deservedly reprinted by the enterprising Club Leabhar in 1969. By his fellow-villagers, Tom Mathieson was nicknamed in turn, Tom the atheist, Tom the serpent and, finally, just "The Philosopher". Tom's story is told in flashback form, but for once the technique does not irritate. The old Philosopher, wandering over his beloved Highland hills one beautiful summer's day, looks back upon his life. He sees himself as a young apprentice in later 19th Century Glasgow being converted to socialism and secularism by his boss, Dougal Robertson. But he has to return home to help his mother on the croft when his father has a heart attack. Tom's father, who is a pillar of the Kirk, is devoutly shocked when he learns of his son's apostasy.

Hallowe'en comes "when the rein is withdrawn from the hallowed, and licence takes the bit in its teeth." Some of the local girls are gathered in the cottage of old Margad who is reputed to be a witch, to participate in the ancient rites of All Hallows' Eve. The boys of the village, including Tom, decide to play a trick on the women. They capture a goat, and drop it down old Margad's chimney hoping it would appear to her and the girls as the very Devil they are worshipping. "Down through the hole came the goat, and landed four-footed in the fire. Its hair went up in a singeing lowe, and with a leap the demented brute was among the wome The girls lost all reason. Two of them fainted. Their screams had a high horror beyond anything that could be imagined. Scream upon scre abject and sickening, so that the knees of the lads went weak and their stomachs flat." The terrified girls burst out of the cottage, and Tom, filled with remorse, catches one of them, Janet Morrison, the daughte of a local merchant who had died of drink, and succeeds in calming her This scene is told with tremendous compassion and tenderness. Tom falls deeply in love with Janet, and for a time it seems she loves him t But when she goes to work as a servant at the Manse, she transfers he affections to Donald Munro, the minister's son.

The discovery of Janet's treachery has a devastating effect on Tom a to try to forget her, he immerses himself in his work. Much against h father's wishes, he sets himself up as a cycle agent in a shop he builds next to the family croft. The business prospers, and during the winter months it is a centre for religious discussion and argument among the youths of the village. One night William Bulbreac, a narrow-minded elder of the Church, enters and accuses Tom of being the Evil one him self. "And the Devil took the shape of a Serpent, for the Devil can take any shape, even your shape you impious blasphemer . . . For I see th serpent within you, I see its evil coils twisting in your body and your brain . . ." Unimpressed by this diatribe, Tom informs Bulbreac that God can't do what even every man can do, namely commit suicide. Whi Tom is delivering himself of this ultimate blasphemy, his father enters the shop. The old man picks up Bulbreac's staff with which to smite hi sacreligious son, but the effort brings on another, and this time fatal, heart attack.

In recalling this tragic episode to his friend the shepherd many years later, the Philosopher admits that "when William Bulbreac called me the serpent he wasn't far wrong. In my own small way I _was_ antiChrist. And the awful thing about the antiChrist is that he has nothing to put in the place of that which he destroys." Nevertheless, the Philosopher goes on to point out that in mythology the serpent by no means always signified the Evil One. "The old Gaelic image of eternity was the wheel made by the serpent when it put its tail in its mouth . . . in the old days the serpent was the symbol of wisdom and of the belief that death came by the woman whose type is the serpent, and that through the same source life comes again. Just as the sun destroys and is the source of life. The Babylonians put a serpent around the heavens."

After his father's death, Tom goes into a decline, and several times he imagines he sees his father's accusing spectre. One day, he learns that Janet is pregnant, and all his old jealousy rekindled, he journeys to Edinburgh with the intention of killing her seducer, Donald Munro, who is a Divinity student there. From this point, the plot takes an improbable melodramatic twist, which is disappointing after the uniform excellence of the preceding chapters. But at the end the Philosopher's peaceful death on a heather-covered slope among his beloved hills is wonderfully described.

The Serpent is a thoughtful novel, the product of a sensitive and highly intelligent mind. The story is consistently interesting and parts of it, particularly Tom's quarrels with his father, make exciting reading. Tom and his mother are convincing creations, and the uneasy, yet essentially loving, relationship between them is subtly brought out.

The chief characters in the highly symbolic The Green Isle of the Great Deep (1944) are a young boy, Art Macrae and an old man, Hector MacDonald who had already figured in Young Art and Old Hector (1942). The latter work consists of a number of strange stories based on ancient Celtic myths and legends (featuring the great Finn MacCoull, Cuchulainn, the Druids, etc.) told by Hector to the fascinated Art. In the former, the two friends become involved in a remarkable series of adventures in a strange land beneath the Hazel Pool into which they both fall while trying to catch a huge salmon.

The country in which they find themselves seems very lush and fertile. They are accosted by a man who says he is a Coastwatcher and they notice that he appears to be "thinking on the surface of his face". He tells them they must report to the "Seat in the North". It will take them three days and three nights to get there and each night they must spend at an inn.

However, Hector and Art decide to sleep in the open, and they feed on the luscious fruit which grows all around. On the third day they are given shelter by a couple, Mary and Robert Campbell, who declare themselves shocked when they learn that Hector and Art have been eating the fruit. But Hector notices that unlike the other inhabitants of the Green Isle the woman seems almost human because she "thinks below the surface of her face". Robert shows them the way to the Seat on the Rock, which turns out to be a fortress not unlike Edinburgh Castle. There they are interviewed by officials who are even more horrified than Robert and Mary when they learn that the friends did not stay at the inns on the way to the Seat and had been eating the fruit. While Hector is being put through a kind of third degree in another part of the fortress, Art manages to escape.

Next morning Hector, after breakfasting on a kind of insipid porridge finds to his surprise that the castle doors and gates are unlocked. He walks out of the building down the street of the village and into the open country. Presently he comes across Art sleeping among some raspberry canes but after eating a few of the raspberries, Hector becomes violently ill. Art wakens and runs to seek help from Robert, who explains that the fruit becomes a poison to the stomach once one has eaten porridge at the inns or at the Seat. He confesses, however, that he and Mary can eat the fruit without harm because she has perfected a herb jelly which neutralises the effect of the poison. The fruit is forbidden says Robert so that "man would be the perfect worker so that he would do all things he was told to do, so that perpetual order would reign everywhere". To the officials at the Seat "obedience is the highest of all virtues for in it is order and seemliness, and an end to the burden of thought and decision. Man's curse has been the curse of disobedience. The fruit is the fruit of life, and those who eat it become imbued with the will to disobey which cannot be tolerated."

After further adventures, Hector is again taken back to the Seat and brought before the most powerful of all the officials who is known as the Questioner. A remorseless interrogation takes place for days and night and eventually Hector reaches the point where "assailed by suggestion from every direction, confession would of itself be desired, would break upon the mind like salvation, even though it meant death. There is a pitch beyond which no burden, no pressure, can be borne. Once the dam is burst, confession comes in a stream, complete and absolute, destroying every barrier, washing away every obstruction." At last, the old man could bear no more, and . . . like some old stag of his native forest he raised his stricken head and stood at bay.

"The Questioner felt a small shiver from that challenge, the whole primordial world stood still, this world and all the universe of men and time.

"And upon this silence, holding the Questioner, by the eyes, old Hector spoke deep out of his throat: 'I want to see God'."

This terrible request is the beginning of the end for the Green Isle. For God created it, has been meditating for thousands of years, and is unaware that its rulers have forsaken wisdom for knowledge. But now, He is awakened, and when Hector is eventually ushered into His presence, He explains that it is for man's salvation essential that wisdom and knowledge be reunited. As legend has it: "The nuts of knowledge must be swallowed by the salmon of wisdom." God tells Hector that there was a time when the Questioner had wisdom. "He used his head and drew on his wisdom. But the more he used his head only, the paler his wisdom became. . . He knew in his head that you suffered, but as the head itself does not suffer, he himself was not affected, for what is affected, swims deep with the salmon. He has divorced knowledge from wisdom, the head from the heart, the intellect from the spirit . . . and because of the divorce, the taste of life has gone bitter, and its hope sterile."

Towards the end the symbolism becomes denser, until the life is almost choked out of the story. But for most of its length, The Green Isle of the Great Deep is a powerful and impressive allegory of totalitarian corruption and brutality. Written during the war, it was, of course, specifically directed against the Nazi tyranny, but its message will remain valid so long as dictators of the Right or the Left try to exercise dominion over the mind of man. Old Hector and Young Art are delightful characters, the former being memorably portrayed during the 60's by that fine actor the late Alex Mackenzie, in the radio adaptation of the novel in dramatic form.

Although The Key of the Chest (1945) is in a sense a "whodunit", it is not recommended to devotees of Agatha Christie or Erle Stanley Gardner who may swiftly become irritated and bored by the subtle psychological probings, and anthropological discussions which so often interrupt the action. The tale is set in an unidentified Highland coastal village in the early years of the century. Charlie MacIan, a failed Divinity student, has had an affair while at Edinburgh University with Flora, the beautiful daughter of the local minister. As a result, Flora is expelled from her college, so that Charlie's relations with her clergyman father are not exactly of the most cordial.

One morning, after a violent storm, Charlie reports that he had found the body of a seaman on the shore around midnight. He claims he carried it to his cottage which he shares with his brother but who, that night, had not returned home because of the wild weather. When found, the seaman was clutching a small cedar-wood chest. However, when the local doctor examines the corpse, he discovers that the seaman did not die of drowning, but of strangulation. Moreover, the chest is locked, and the key is missing. Suspicion falls on Charlie, and he and Flora disappear . . .

A considerable part of the novel is occupied with discussions on primitive religion and customs between Michael Sandeman the laird, Mr. Gwyn a literary man and philosopher, and the doctor. Great stress is laid on the integrated life of primitive peoples, which the modern world has completely split, if not destroyed. But the ultimate outlook is hopeful, because man is naturally good. There is also the suggestion of the incestuous relationship between the minister and Flora . . .

On the whole, in spite of the author's skill and keen psychological insight, the characters somehow remain unrealised. Moreover, the diffus pantheistic mysticism at the heart of the novel fails to convince. To com pensate, however, there are some stunningly beautiful passages and som striking turns of phrase: "Fate stood quiet as an alien fisherman among them . . . The wind ran about the heather, like a soft-mouthed spaniel seeking a scent."

When The Drinking Well (1947) opens, the hero Iain Cattanach, is in his last year at school in a Highland town. His father is an impoverishe sheep farmer and his mother is determined that Iain shall not follow in his footsteps. She goes to see the factor, Major Grant, who promises to try to secure a post for Iain with an Edinburgh firm of solicitors. Iain at first refuses, as his heart is set on sheep-farming, but after his mothe dies of cancer, he reluctantly agrees to enter the lawyer's office. Before leaving, he pays a visit to the local witch, Mad Mairag. Near her croft there is an old drinking well, and Mairag tells him that the children are "frightened of the feet that go there", though Iain knows the well is used only by Mairag herself.

Iain soon settles down into the routine of the office, though he finds city life alien and oppressive. However, he has a love affair with the lovely Morna Galloway, secretary to his boss, and intellectually comes under the influence of a brilliant man named Douglas, a fervent Scottish Nationalist. But he falls foul of an unpleasant fellow-clerk Smeaton, and one day in the course of a furious argument, he throws Smeaton bodily through the glass door of the office. Feeling sure this will mean the end of his career, he walks out and catches the first available train back to his hometown. His father thinks he is ill, and Iain does not disillusion him, though he knows it must only be a matter of time before the truth i revealed. It is early spring, and in spite of his father's protests, Iain insists on going to a farm three miles distant to bring home the hoggs after the winter weathering. On the way back he is caught in a violent snowstorm and is given up for dead. . .

The novel is very readable, and apart from the drinking well itself, whose pure uncontaminated waters clearly represent life, there is little of the familiar Gunn symbolism. Unfortunately, following Iain's return from Edinburgh, the story becomes absurdly novelettish, and were it not so well-written, might easily have appeared as a serial in The People's Friend. The underlining of the contrast between Iain's two loves, the sophisticated city girl Morna, and the simple Highland lassie Mary, seems to have been done many times before. The characters, too appear drearily familiar, the wayward but essentially decent hero, the old woman whose "madness" is really a very profound form of sanity, the sneering artificial city gent, and so on. In the end, all the misunderstandings are as miraculously resolved as in any product of Hollywood's vintage years.

Nevertheless, there is some stunning descriptive writing (e.g. of Edinburgh's Royal Mile) and the arguments for Scottish Home Rule are marshalled and presented with tremendous power and conviction, recalling those in the first part of Compton Mackenzie's "North Wind of Love".

The Shadow (1948) is set in a village in the Scottish Highlands during the Second World War. Nan Gordon is convalescing in the house of her Aunt Phemie from a nervous breakdown brought about by her gruelling experiences during the London blitz. These make up the shadow from which she must escape, if she is to get well. One day an old man is found murdered in a lonely cottage in the area. The police suspect that a shell-shocked local man, Gordon MacMaster who has disappeared is responsible. While walking in the woods Nan makes the acquaintance of an artist, Adam MacAlpine, by whom she is both repelled and attracted. They begin to meet often, but one day in a lonely place on the other side of the mountain, he tries to assault her. In the struggle, she fights away from him to the edge of a loch and there, at their feet, is the drowned bloated body of Gordon MacMaster . . .

Nan discovers to her horror that the shadow has pursued her from London, and to try to protect herself, she relapses again into severe depression. In alarm, Aunt Phemie sends for Ronald Surrey, a Communist with whom Nan had been very friendly in London. Enraged by Nan's story, Ronald goes in search of Adam and discovers him painting a waterfall from the other side of a gorge. They fight, and Adam falls over the edge . . . Though this summary might suggest that The Shadow is a simple tale of murder, attempted rape and revenge, it is, in fact, a subtle psychological study of the three chief characters, Nan, Ronald and Aunt Phemie. It is cunningly constructed, the whole of the first part consisting of a series of rather cryptic letters from Nan to Ronald. The pattern of the plot does not clearly emerge until Ronald arrives from London (from which point the story is told straightforwardly in the third person), but readers should not be deterred by the allusive difficult nature of the opening section as some considerable treasures lie in store. Nevertheless, the first third of the novel is certainly heavy-going. With typical secretiveness, Gunn does not let us know the heroine's age till Page 25, nor her first name till Page 41. But his main lesson, that even the most apparently rational person is at times governed by unconscious primeval forces beyond his control, and that this fact must be recognised before any definitive philosophy of life is formulated, is driven home forcefully and clearly enough. Nan recognises that Ronald, the seemingly remorselessly logical Communist, is in grave danger of forgetting love and compassion, and becoming like Kronos, who, according to the Greek myth, devoured his own children.

"For Nan, Kronos was not a devouring father in the literal image, but just a slayer of sons, of young men. He was the dictator who purged and killed whenever he saw a threat to his authority. The new multiple-Kronos of the world Nan had experienced in war, in the street. He stood for the destructiveness which, in Nan's world today would, in order to achieve its clear rational aim, coldly ignore emotion . . . and so, inevitably and fatally destroy life. To achieve, he would multiply himself and kill." This was the shadow which Nan had to destroy or be destroyed herself.

All who are interested in psycho-analysis and in the actiology and cure of mental illness will find this an absorbing and illuminating novel.

In The Silver Bough (1948), Gunn restates his belief in the prehistoric Golden Age of carefree primitive hunting people who inhabited the hills and glens of what is now Scotland before the Celts and Gaels arrived to bedevil the scene.

Simon Grant, an archaeologist, comes to a village in the Scottish Highlands to excavate a chambered cairn surrounded by a circle of standing stones situated in the property of a local landowner, Donald Martin. Martin gives him permission to begin digging, but is at no pains to conceal his hostility towards archaeology, which he clearly regards as an essentially negative and destructive pursuit. To assist him, Grant is able only to enlist the help of Andie Mackenzie the village natural - a fine character sketch this. However, Andie turns out to be a good and willing worker. Simon finds lodgings with old Mrs. Cameron, whose granddaughter Anna, though unmarried, has a small daughter Sheena. One night, he hears Mrs. Cameron tell Sheena the story of the silver bough. This was the branch of an apple tree from which there hung nine golden apples, and which, when it was shaken, collided with one another to produce the sweetest music ever heard. Simon conceives the idea of writing to Edinburgh to ask if a craftsmen friend of his could fashion a silver bough which would play a melody, like the one in the legend.

The excavation of the cairn begins, and soon a coffin is unearthed in which repose the skeletons of a mother and her child. Simon feels that in some obscure mythical way they are connected with Anna and Sheena. Some days later, he finds an urn in which there is a horde of gold - "the crock at the foot of the rainbow" in fairy lore. But while he is examining it in his room, foolish Andie bursts in and knocks him unconscious. When he recovers, both Andie and the urn have gone.

The rest of the novel is concerned with Grant's attempts to find out

where Andie has hidden the urn, and with exploring the strange relationship between Anna, Martin and Sheena. Is Martin Sheena's father?
Reluctantly, Grant grows to respect and even like Martin with his "neolithic face, his stillness, his strength and his inner integrity of being".
He discovers that due to a traumatic experience in the Far East during
the war, Martin has lost all faith in humanity and is bent on self-destruc-
tion. "He can be cured only through being reborn." Can this perhaps be
accomplished through the innocent unconscious therapy of little Sheena
who has been transfigured with delight and wonder since her very own
silver bough arrived from Simon's craftsman friend?

As has been said, Gunn in this novel reiterates his conviction that
modern man's predicament has its roots in ancient myths which are
re-enacted in his dreams, and albeit unconsciously, in many of his actions. One feels, however, that the author was not too clear in his own
mind about the connection of the various legends both with each other,
and with his creations, so that his ultimate conclusions remain obscure.
The complex character of Martin is presented with subtlety and insight,
but plot-tension is lacking, and the novel will chiefly be enjoyed by those
with an interest in the technicalities of archaeological and anthropological
research.

The Lost Chart (1949) is a complicated story of espionage and counter-
espionage set in the period of the "cold war" between Russia and the West
in the late 'forties.

Dermot Cameron, who is an agent for British Intelligence, is given the
chart of the Hebridean island of Claddy where, during the war, he had
been engaged in espionage investigations. While walking along a city
street, he sees a young woman apparently being attacked by two men.
He runs to her aid but in the struggle the chart disappears. The damsel
turns out to be Christina McNeil whom Dermot had met in Claddy when
she was a little girl. Her reappearance reawakens in him guilt feelings
in connection with the death of her grandfather, a coastwatcher on the
island. He discovers that Christina is living with people whom Intelligence believe are working for the Communist Secret Service. Dermot's
attempts to recover the chart almost cost him his life, and presently he
begins to suspect, like Michael Caine in some spy film drama of the 60's,
that his own superiors are as indifferent to his survival as are his antagonists.

The old problem of whether the end ever justifies the means is central
to this novel. Dermot realises that as a police spy he must often behave
in a thoroughly despicable manner, but concludes that the triumph of
Communism would mean even more police, and secret ones at that.
When The Lost Chart was written, a 3rd world war seemed almost in-

evitable, and most of the discussions reflect the pessimism and even despair felt by thinking men of that period. It is interesting to note that the book appeared in the same year as George Orwell's celebrated prophecy of doom, "Nineteen Eighty-four".

Like that of many spy films the plot of The Lost Chart is not easy to follow, and even the most avid addict of the genre may eventually get lost in its endless convolutions. Most of the characters are shadowy and ill-formed, even Dermot's mistress, a Gaelic folk-singer, remaining curiously undeveloped. However, there is a clever tragi-comic cameo of Mrs. Spicer, a one-time suffragette, and a subtle psychological portrait of Joe Duguid, an idealistic artist (somewhat reminiscent of Dostoyevsky's Prince Mishkin) who becomes Dermot's rival for the heart of the fair Christina. The sentimentality which, from The Drinking Well onwards, unfortunately begins to be writ more and more large in Gunn's novels, disfigures the concluding chapters of this one.

The Well at the World's End (1951) is a highly symbolic account of a middle-aged Professor of History's search for meaning and truth while on a holiday in the Scottish Highlands.

One "well" is introduced in the first pages of the novel, when Professor Peter Munro and his wife Fand are directed to it by an old woman and find its water "so crystal clear that it appeared not to be there". At that moment, Peter is convinced that he must set out to find the something in life that we think isn't there - "the well at the world's end". Fand reminds him that in Gaelic legend, a goddess who hoped to discover in the well the land of youth, knowledge and poetry, was engulfed by its waters and drowned. Nevertheless, Peter sets out on his mission because, as he tells Fand 'if ever there was a time we could be doing with that well, it's now".

The remainder of the novel is occupied with Peter's many adventures during his travels. He investigates a haunted cottage with almost tragic results, he falls in with a merry crowd of illicit whisky distillers, he re-encounters an old friend Cocklebuster (for whom there were "no well at the world's end . . . nor anything that went through boundaries; for Cocklebuster was as sane as a cliché") and he witnesses the remarkable reawakening of a soured husband's love for his wife through the magical power of the "mothan", the pearlwort of the mountains. Finally, on his way back to Fand he falls over a cliff while trying to rescue a lamb stranded on a ledge. Is this the end, or has he at last discovered the object of his quest?

Gunn's basic message in this allusive and difficult novel, is that only by forgetting self can man paradoxically discover his true Self. At this period Gunn was greatly under the influence of Zen Buddhism and the psychology of Dr. C.G. Jung. There is much interesting discussion of the subject in the Atom of Delight. Peter is continually being faced during his travels with the choice between the easy way of self-gratification or the hard way of self-naughting. He is always impelled eventually to choose the latter, and his final joyful realisation is that Tir-nan Og, the land of youth, is attainable here and now and does not lie at the foot of the well at the world's end. This, of course, is the essence of Zen teaching. Many of the familiar Gunn symbols reappear here - the pure uncontaminated water of innocence, the serpent sucking its own tail, the hazelnuts of knowledge, signifying the inability of human reason to apprehend ultimate truth, and so on. Supernaturalism and the illusory nature of time are also again strongly emphasised - indeed sometimes Peter feels he is travelling backwards, and that when he gets back to Fand he will be "a child in arms at the beginning of the world".

Although the novel contains much creative and imaginative writing of a very high order, some of the episodes are embarrassingly sentimental and melodramatic. Moreover in parts it is so unintelligible that it will necessarily appeal only to a specialised clientèle, even among those interested in Zen, and Jungian psychology. As C.E.M. Joad once pointed out, there is a difference between the expression of obscurity and obscurity of expression, and in this work, one wonders sometimes if Gunn is really trying to utter the unutterable or if the obscurity is simply due to faulty craftsmanship.

In the same year, however, (1951) Gunn published a volume of short stories entitled The White Hour which contains some of his finest writing.

"Whistle for Bridge" is, construction-wise, a model of its kind. Intending practitioners of the art should note the wealth of information which is unobtrusively given in the first few paragraphs. This enchanting little story captures perfectly all the wonder and heartbreak which can occur in the life of a sensitive child. Though verging on the sentimental, "The Old Man" is a compassionate and touching tale about an aged gypsy who, Solomon-like, solves the emotional problems of the members of his clan. In the delightful "Paper Boats", Gunn seems to be teaching that variety is, indeed, the spice of life. The perfect boat owned by George "seemed to have no sport of her own, and her dead perfection floated listlessly broadside on", but Hugh's little craft was "oddly alive as though it delighted in its imperfection".

The coming of death as a friend to those advanced in years is a recurring motif in the collection - e.g. in the stark and tragic "Symbolical", "Some Stuff as Dreams" and "Down to the Sea", which all describe with profound compassion the "slipping of the moorings" by the elderly. In the latter, an old fisherman elects joyfully to die in the sea, around which his entire life had revolved. With fine irony, the opening sentence of the story records the remark of a friend at his funeral: 'It'd have been better for him, mebbe, if they had put him to the poorhouse.'

"The Tax Gatherer" and "Henry Drake Goes Home" are both about the human side of bureaucracy. The "washing of the hands" symbolism in the former is perhaps a little too obvious, but the latter is a beautifully told, heart-warming story concerning an English old age pensioner livir in Caithness who sets out during the war to walk to his home in Devon where he wants to die. His progress is followed by the sympathetic official who had arranged many years previously for the delivery of the old man's first pension.

"The Black Woollen Gloves" describes the delicate relationship which develops between a young student who leaves his gloves in a public library, and the girl who finds them. The surprise ending is a delight. "The Mirror" is a taut satirical account of how an artist realises his ow limitations while on a visit to a Highland croft. In "Pure Chance", one o the characters tells the narrator that "In Arduan you don't run after a girl . . . you do your best in secret and delicate ways and then nature, thriving in this kind of game, arranges that chance throws you together naturally. This happens and can be very exciting."

"The Ghost's Story" is told by a spook who fought for the Earl of Moray at Stirling Bridge and Bannockburn where he is killed. Grand Scottish Nationalist propaganda this, and proof that Gunn can write in a straightforward no-nonsense manner when he so desires. In the powerfully satirical "Montrose Rides By", an indomitable Inverness tavern-keeper caught between the warring armies of Montrose and Argyle, fights to save her property. The description of the defeated Montrose entering the town is told with sharply-pointed irony.

At the beginning of Gunn's next full-length novel, Bloodhunt (1952), Allan Innes murders Robert Menzies at a dance in a small Highland town because he has impregnated Allan's former sweetheart, Liz Murison, and is refusing to marry her. He flees into the hills and is pursued by Robert's brother, Nicol, the local policeman. For Nicol the operation is more than the bringing to justice of a killer, it is a bloodhunt.

Allan takes refuge on an artificial island in a remote loch, and is befriended and given food and occasional shelter by Old Sandy, a retired seaman, now a crofter. One day Sandy has an accident, and a neighbour comes to look after him. Old Sandy fears that if she stays the night Allan will appear, and be discovered. To his relief she at last agrees t his pleas that she return to her own home, but at ten o'clock that same evening, Liz Murison, big with child, appears at his door seeking asylu having been turned out by her own parents. Meanwhile Nicol, now half-crazed with the desire to avenge his brother's death, continues his remorseless search for the fugitive. . .

This novel, one of Gunn's best, takes place within the space of about ten days. It is tautly constructed, and the suspense is well sustained throughout. But it is much, much more than an exciting thriller though it can certainly be read and enjoyed simply on that level. It is also a profound allegory of Cain the hunted and Christ the Saviour, "the only two immortal stories of all those invented by man".

The plot pivots around the finely-observed character of Old Sandy, who like Old Hector in The Green Isle of the Great Deep is a Highlander of the most admirable type, kindly, courageous and completely incorruptible. The relationship which develops between Sandy and young Liz Murison is told movingly but without the sentimentality which mars The Well at the World's End, and there is much delightful humour as well as wisdom in the arguments Sandy has with the local minister. The novel's main thesi: that, as one character puts it, "No man gets away with his reckoning but with luck he may learn how to face it" is convincingly and effectively put across.

The plot of Gunn's last novel to date The Other Landscape (1954) some what recalls that of The Silver Bough. The narrator, Willie Urquhart, a: anthropologist, arrives at a remote West Highland hotel to seek out Dougla Menzies, author of a typescript entitled "Cliffs", which he has submitted to a magazine edited by a friend of Urquhart's. Both Urquhart and his friend agree it is a work of genius. Menzies turns out to be a deep, com plex character who, with only a savage dog for company, has lived a her-mit-like existence in a white-washed cottage since the death of his belov-ed wife, Annabel, a year or so previously.

Menzies is at first hostile, but gradually a strange friendship develops between him and Urquhart. Menzies is engaged on a spiritual quest for the "wrecker" who destroys the young and innocent, and who inhabits "the other country" beyond this where "labels" or "symbols" rather than logi-cal concepts apply. As Urquhart describes it in the novel:

. . . "Then he, (Menzies) said something which had an instant and extraordinary effect on me. It was as though our talk in its loops and twists had been a mysterious build-up for his final sentence.

"'God's ways are non-rational' he said, 'either non-rational, or there is no God. Were it otherwise, did God exist and were He rational, then his doings would be susceptible of a logical exposition. His horrors wouldn't call for faith. So if there is a God, he must have a different system.'

"It had the shock of an insight for me at that moment and words vanished . . . And then I knew . . . that for Menzies, the penetration of the other system was now all that mattered."

Urquhart also falls in love with Catherine McGregor, a local girl wl is at University, but who is working as a chambermaid at the hotel du ing her holidays. The slender plot deals chiefly with the intricate rel. tions between Urquhart, Menzies and Catherine, but it is the dead Ann bel who dominates the story rather in the manner of Rebecca in Daphn du Maurier's celebrated romance. Sometimes, Menzies' vision of Annabel is so strong that it is projected outside of himself and the oth "see" her too.

Although the supernatural atmosphere is well established, the vario strands in the narrative somehow do not knit into a coherent whole. There are fine individual character studies of a choleric major, a gue at the hotel and his enemy, William McGregor, a gillie (Catherine's father) and "Sam Mor" (Big Sam) the manager, but their connection wit the central theme is obscure. Catherine herself is far too saintly a heroine to be credible or even interesting, and the ending is both melo dramatic and sentimental. Nevertheless, The Other Landscape has much to offer those who have a taste for profound metaphysical discus ions conducted by articulate civilized people. Once again, it illustrat Gunn's deep distrust of those who attempt to create logical systems, a his belief that ultimate reality can only be apprehended directly in a m ment of time.

Neil Gunn is a novelist of great sensitivity and intelligence. He can satirical (though never cruelly so), tender and romantic, witty and pro foundly serious. He has a wide knowledge of sheep-farming, fishing (especially poaching!) and country life in general. His worst faults ar his sentimentality (there is more than a trace of the kailyard in The Drinking Well and The Well at the World's End) and his obscurity, whe the thread of his plot sometimes become lost in a thicket of symbols. On a few occasions, the unintelligibility seems almost wilful, but usua it is due to the difficult nature of his subject-matter which often is con cerned with regions where, as Gunn himself is continually stressing, logical concepts do not apply. As Walter Urquhart puts it to Douglas Menzies inThe Other Landscape: "The reader feels that the writer has experienced with an intense clarity of vision what he, the reader, can see only as in a glass darkly, the degree of darkness being in inverse ratio to the intuitive insight." This sums up perfectly the thoughtful reader's reaction to Gunn. He has a hauntingly beautiful style which only very occasionally is rich to the point of indigestibility. His re current images are often startling and original, and always wonderful expressed. Few writers in Scotland, or elsewhere, have been able to describe storms at sea with such breath-taking power and versatility as those in <u>Morning Tide</u> and <u>The Silver Darlings</u>.

Gunn has also the ability to create memorable characters, being particularly skilful in portraying sensitive young boys and wise old men. Though he is not strictly speaking a Highlander himself, his deep respect and love for the Highland ethos are expressed again and again in his novels. The Highlanders' deep integrity, their innate dignity, and their hospitality towards strangers are continually emphasised. In <u>The Well at the World's End</u> he describes how many Highlanders never lock their doors at night lest Christ, in the guise of a stranger, should come seeking refreshment and shelter. In their eyes, the greatest crime is the betrayal of a friend. Gunn shares too the Highlanders' belief in second sight and precognition.

Gunn makes few concessions to the lazy reader, and though some of his novels are concerned, as we have seen, with murder and espionage, they will not appeal to those who seek mindless entertainment and cheap thrills. But for the reader who is prepared to make a little effort, the rewards are great indeed. There is no doubt that Neil Gunn is in the very front rank in the field of twentieth century Scottish fiction, and that his novels, dealing as they do with universal and timeless themes, will still be read and enjoyed when those of most of his contemporaries have long been forgotten.

Dunbeath Castle

NEIL M. GUNN RECORDER AND INTERPRETER

Francis Thompson

It is one of the functions (one might even suggest duty) of writers to express in their work their nationhood, that complicated weave of history, tradition, attitudes and opinions which make up a nation. They should serve as the articulate members of their society to project a true and honest image of their fellows. There should also be an honest interpretation of the life around them, as it goes on around the writer in the present, or went on in the accessible immediate past. Some areas in Scotland have been reasonably well served by writers, and the Highlands have been more than fortunate in having Neil M. Gunn to perform a kind of public relations service on behalf of the region which is only beginning to become appreciated by a new and wider audience.

The Highlands and Islands have never been noted for their production of writers of stature. Certainly, in the Gaelic context, there were literary giants. But Gaelic has at the present time a poor and scanty readership. An edition of prose of 1000 copies is fortunate if it is sold within a year or so. An edition of 2000 copies is a waste of good paper.

As it is, only two writers have emerged to produce work in English about the region: Neil Munro and Neil Gunn. Munro had the gleam of genius in his work, but it shone through with all the mystery of a Celtic light that any who followed its path would end up in Erehwon in a land of romance and rapture, where enchantment grips the soul like a clam and the mind's edges become blunt and unable to discern reality from imagination.

Gunn, on the other hand, possessed the ability to take a firm hold on the Celtic tradition to which he fell heir and shape it so that it became a recognisable part of his writing. One would say that Gunn is in the true line of the great Gaelic bards, in that, through the medium of the English language, he has carried on what they themselves fell heir to in their turn and in their time. Gunn is at his best when describing the natural scene, and one has no hesitation in comparing him to Duncan Ban MacIntyre.

There is also a genuine element of realism in Gunn's work. George Blake wrote in 1959: ' ... those of us (Neil Gunn, Eric Linklater, Bruce Marshall, Lewis Grassic Gibbon, James Barke and Neil Paterson) who started writing during the 1920's - 30's did lift the novel back to a truer relationship to a contemporary life. This might appear to indicate a bias on my part towards realism and the documentary. If so, forget it. It seems to be inevitable, however, that the Scottish Novel, in the queer topographical and racial circumstances we live in, is bound to be regional - unless you are the genius who is going to pick up all the threads, weave them into a coherent pattern and present the ethos in its entirety.'

Gunn has the remarkable gift of being able to portray the Highlands and Highlanders on two levels in a manner which was original and which it is doubtful if it can ever be repeated.

The first level is the authentic description of the physical environmen in which the Highlander has always lived out his life. It was, and to a large extent still is, a significant environment which moulded his character and his way of thinking. Gunn's portrayal of it has added an extra dimension of appreciation for the sympathetic reader who has also been offered a deeper insight into the Highland makeup.

The second level is that elevated plane above normal on which the Highland and Celtic mind seems so able to operate with fluent ease. Again Gunn has used his gift of words and the facility of his pen to paint an honest portrait of this inner world of the Highlander. It is a world which is unseen, yet which is obvious, almost tangible, to the reader who accepts Gunn's text on its designed level.

There are many instances in the corpus of Gunn's literary output to show how excellent he is in the role of a recorder and interpreter of the Highland scene. This aspect of his work is one which has, to my knowledge, rarely if ever been touched upon. Yet Gunn himself has pointed to it many times.

In an essay in Saltire Review (No. 19, Autumn 1959) entitled 'Landscape Inside', Gunn says: 'A novelist cannot write about people in a vacuum. They must have a background, and the background becomes part of them, conditioning to some extent almost everything they do. When this works at a fairly deep level, it can be quite unconscious. I can't remember (though I may be wrong) ever having described a Highland scene for the scene's sake. Always the scene had something to do with the mind of the character who found himself there. The difference here is like the difference between a colour photograph of a landscape and an artist's painting of it. In the painting, the artist, with his kind of mind, is present. In the colour photograph no mind is present. Per- haps this explains why so many set descriptions of scenes, like sunsets, can be boring, or why lovely Highland glens, shot in colour film, have sometimes been dubbed picture-postcardy by critics. However, let me stick for the moment to the novelist, who does in fact often describe the mood of a character by describing the background, the physical scene. Or vice versa. There is a sort of oblique traffic between the two, and this can thicken the texture of both. When the character, for example, is on top of the world, the world becomes a wonderful place. When he is feeling depressed or nihilistic then the world around him becomes detached and uncaring. When one hears a critic describing the background as the principal character in a novel, it means that the background is actively dictating the character. This can often happen in the Highland

And later: ' ... unless you come upon yourself in some such way, a an element present in the scene or landscape, the chances are that you will forget it, however long you look at it. And I suspect the artist's exercise of looking three separate times was not only to observe the detail, which is essential, but to give this special kind of awareness a chance to happen. It can be magical and memorable when it does, and only when it does.'

While it would be more than possible to write at great length about Gunn's ability to merge scene and character into a recognisable whole, it is much better to allow Gunn to do this for himself, for no critical analysis could hope to present fully his inborn genius for being that kin of artist who records and interprets at the same time to produce a moment full of the magical and enthralling qualities of which he himself ha written.

In 'Half-Light', <u>The White Hour</u>, there is a picture which illustrates admirably how the observer of a scene gradually merges with what he sees to become an essential part of it, a hub of life and active thought which produces an experience which is almost soul-consuming and one which must be undergone to be fully appreciated in all its aspects.

' ... The tall grey salmon-net poles got me tonight. They stood ther in that bunch near enough together, so that you could almost spit from one to the other; yet tonight each seemed lonely and thin and wrapped up in a grey self-consuming. 'Apart' is the word. Good Lord — 'apart Yet there it is. These bits of grey weather-cracked poles! And they got me with a sense of kinship, so that I stood among them until my hearing and sight became abnormally acute and my body stiff. From their little green plateau you look down on the harbour basin. It is empty. Look long enough - it fills. Oh, I know it is imagination, that I am allowing my starry eyes to see things. Obviously there is nothing nothing material. There is merely this much: the place has its 'influence'. By way of experiment, I have given way to this influence once o twice. I give way again. A certain hypnotic, sinking sensation ...

'The harbour basin fills. Boat-decks, rigging, masts slanting to res in their crutches, figures moving about, at first dimly, then more distinctly; a face, faces; sounds: all coming before the staring eyes through stages, as it were, of imperfect focussing, till the picture lives, moves, throbs. A species of 'movies' if you like - for away from the influence one must joke about it to keep balance. But under the influence - my father's stride, a trifle quicker than the others; the face a trifle more alert; the tongue with its ever ready shaft. And there his men from the Lews - the heave-ho! chant of the voices, the krik! krik! of the halyards as the mast goes slowly aloft. The brown sails - there they go slipping past the quay-wall to breast the sea: out of the smooth harbour basin to this restless dipping and rising and gliding of the great brown-winged seabirds they are. The smother of life left behind, the ripe richness of the young women-gutter's faces, the smiling wrinkles of the old, the incredibly deft fingers, the talk, the laughter, the work.

'An ache comes to the soul, the lips stir to an old savour, salty, brimful of life. Something here of the marrow. School-keeping, shop-keeping, book-clerking, all the pale, anaemic occupations of landsmen and city men, dear Lord - how ghastly! their passion a hectic spurting, their contentment a grey haze. Teaching children all day long so that they may 'get on', may be successful in attaining the clerical stool or pulpit, or in measuring, at a profit, so many yards of red flannel for a country woman's needs. And being polite always: it pays. God!

'Am I a throw-back, am I? All this centred in me as the living evocation of the dead sea-board?

'Perhaps my very hate of this place is but a sort of wrong-headed, savage worship? What a damned juggling with perhapses!'

In this passage Gunn reveals his insight into an aspect of Highland character which indicates perhaps a personal experience: that of the relationship between the exile and his homeplace.

There are many types of expatriate Highlander, possibly typified by the person whose wrenching out by the roots from his homeplace by imposed economic and social processes has created a bitter reaction, like the snapping of a brain-cord. The original, natural love of the homeplace gives way to a vehement rejection of all those values that had taken a thousand years in their making. The old culture, its brave stand against the sophisticated (i.e., corrupted) attitudes and opinions of a heartless and insentient urbanised civilisation, is seen in ridicule, in a stage caricature, yet is a circus clown who, but for the want of seeing eyes and hearing ears, portrays the true realities of life in all its forms of harshness.

At the same time, the schizophrenic expatriate seeks to protect and preserve his origins by associating with expatriate bodies which exist, almost like pinpricks, in densely-populated conurbations, and whose

aims are primarily the fossilisation of Highland culture and the values
it has generated, forgetting that these same values exist simultaneous
with each attempt to preserve it in the surviving communities of the
homeplace.

The process of fossilisation is regularly checked out against reality
by references back to the homeplace: the return home for a holiday to
reinforce the view that 'the place is really dead and we are well out of
it'; the participation in distorted social patterns and movements such a
ceilidhs; the self-gratification which results from a deep-sinking into a
morass of sweet comfort and luxurious self-pitying expression of cloy-
ing nostalgia in the writing of an exilic poem or song.

Occasionally, the expatriate realises that something undefinable is
owed by him to the community and a return is made in the form of
minister or schoolmaster, a position of high social position which shed
lustre on the community that threw him up. But once there, the mind
becomes opiated with an overwhelming sense of belonging, a 'home aga
sense which almost completely blots out the practical reasons which initiated the return. In the end, the once-estranged product of the comm
unity reverts to nature, as does a rod of iron in the ground when it reverts back to the form in which it is found in nature, to leave only tant-
ilising traces of its former processed shape and properties.

All this is seen in a number of Gunn's works. In Gunn's short story,
"Half Light" we have the uncomfortable feeling that Gunn is the psychia-
trist and one is lying on the leather couch, performing the ritual of
analysis. With a rare insight into the psyche of the Highlander, he has
spoken, from a personal experience, for countless others who lack his
articulation, logic and ability to look deep within themselves to discover
both what makes them tick and what in fact is the root cause of the miss
ed heartbeats whenever they are confronted with the seemingly diametri
ally-opposed reality of the southern city and that same reality of life and
living which exists in the rural communities of the Highlands and Island

'His vehemence had startled me. "I tell you I wouldn't go back there
no, not though it meant a fortune ... The place is dead, man! It's done
Good God, it's full of ghosts! The little harbours are silting up, the
curing sheds are roofless, the boats are gone ... What are the few
crofts but crouching, squatting brute things - dead, too, by heaven!'
... My dear chap, who's the decadent? Do I go reading all that sort of
stuff you do? Do I have anything to do with Celtic Twilight or quattro-
centists or any life-at-second-hand business of that sort? You enjoy
that; I don't - no more than I do the grey wastes - yonder.'

In The Drinking Well, a book in which the heart of Scotland speaks to
all who are conscious of their national identity, there is an interesting

passage which links the expatriate with his homeplace. This book was one of the first of Gunn's works which the present writer found so absorbing that it has held its memory fast in my mind over a period of some two decades.

Iain Cattanach is listening to a speaker at the Mound in Edinburgh:

'And who is going to do that for us in the Highlands to-day?' asked the ironic questioner.

'Listen', answered the speaker. 'Have you noticed that you asked who is going to do that for us? Not - how are we ourselves going to do it? In the very form of your question you exhibit the fatal psychology which has landed us where we are, and which, in particular, has landed the Highlands where they are. No wonder the women of the Highlands drive their clever sons from home, into offices, into school teaching, into pulpits where they can comfortably wag their pows, anywhere - so long as it is off the land, for which their menfolk refuse to fight. Not, perhaps, that we can altogether blame the men. For who would support them in the fight? Would London, whose financiers rent the deer forests? ... But - had there been our own men here, to support us in our fight on croft and hill and sea, then the story might indeed have been a very different and gallant one, for, given a cause and a lead, the Highlanders have shown themselves among the great fighters of the world. They showed it in the Great War. It could still be a gallant fight - and a successful one ... '

Given a cause and a lead ... In The Key of the Chest, Gunn indicates to us what it means to be one of those who show some measure of faith in a community, to the extent of trying to bring a relevancy and contemporary aspect into it.

'No one knew, as Kenneth did, how much diplomacy and careful agitation, how much thought and sheer labour, it had taken to get hold of the Ros and start the sheep club. How often he had been near throwing the whole thing up! The jealousies, the trifling doubts!

'But he had done it. And, dammit, he would do more. He would get the mails contract. He would organise the collecting and transport of lobsters in his own vans. And people were saying that some day there would be motor vans, even in the Highlands. He would make money out of this place, and if they did not come with him, the harder he would screw them.

'But he must watch that softness in himself, the welling up of the mood, the friendliness that laughed in the moment and for the moment's sake, that weakness.

'... A man owed his community something. Kenneth Grant had said that one or two men, like Norman and Charlie, could be leaders who would put the place once more on its feet. It was something like that that was needed. Belief that they could do things for themselves had got lost. Not only lost here, but lost in every small place of the world like it. But here there was something worth finding again. A too rigid religion and what not may have helped to blot it out, but it was worth finding again, a whole way of life that had bred fine men and women, kind-hearted, strong, decent.

' ... they were the people of the community, and they had their way of living, the right way and the wrong way, distilled out of numberless ages, so that the right way and the wrong way became native to the blood, like an instinct, known also to the very birds and animals that lived together, this conscience, this thing which needed no words was - morality'.

There is much thorough-going descriptive work in <u>Butcher's Broom</u>. The whole book in fact becomes like a roomful of old memories, brought back to a semblance of reality, displaying a form of their old original environment from whence they were taken in their own times. There is a great storehouse of wealth and detail here, of life, of living, of attuning to the processes of Nature to which Man must always accept or die. There is also evidence of Gunn's thorough absorption of both the myth and reality of the ancient and immediate past history of the Highlands. He gives an intimate picture of real people, their attitudes to their circumstances. One sees their eyes open at the wonder of a surprise; the gleam of pride in them as the salmon is caught; the terror in a drawn face as fate takes the unexpected turn and the dice rolls to a standstill at impending death or disaster; the calmness of an expected death, when the life goes from the body in a white light that propels itself, as all spirits should be allowed to do, in a hesitant movement towards the open window to mingle with the airs of the moorland and seashore; the look in the wonder of love of one person for another; the whole magic of realising one-self in the context of others; the helplessness that comes over one like a black swoon as the inevitable crouches at the open door to spring at one's throat to tear it out and cause the heart to burst with the effort of fright.

One always has the tendency to describe Gunn as a 'quiet' writer, the silent onlooker on the touchline of life who sees, with the nodding of an understanding head, the essentials of life, almost static, yet, like the very centre of a rotating hub, full of vitality. Even when he describes wild scenes - the wildness and cruelty of nature, and the desperate clashes between human beings - there is the ever-present Gunn hovering over the disarray. But one has to read and re-read to appreciate fully the wide-ranging canvas represented by his literary output. Like motifs in a Sibelius symphony, so are the glimpses of Gunn in each of his works. Gunn can be appreciated only if taken as a whole, as the eye must take in the garden of a Zen monastery, defining the perimeters and relating the pattern and symmetry to allow the mind to distil the images into a simple thought.

Gunn's recording techniques make one think of the film documentary - the fact as seen by the mechanical eye of the camera from an interpretive angle dictated by the instinct of Gunn the director. He is there in a desperate climb up a cliff-face after seabirds' eggs. He is there among the herring-gutters on long wooden quays as they plunge their bloodied hands into the long wooden troughs full of the harvest of silver darlings, fresh, glinting in the sun with the shimmer of the scintillating sea still on their dulling scales. He is there as the camera zooms in to watch the gutting knife cut its way around and about each fish, enduring this last rite with a stoic look, before it is thrown to the packers and salters standing by their fresh-wood-staved iron-bound barrels. His ear directs the microphone to pick up for the sound track of the film, the voices and the sounds of the quayside scene.

He is there, too, standing on a low, heather-covered knoll, grass crinkling beneath his feet, looking over and above the mottled moors, absorbing the ancient tale which the land in the Highlands has ever ready on its lips to tell the hearing ear. He is there looking up at an eternal sea-sky, moody, reflecting the immense vitality of the moving waters beneath it, breathing as if in a deep sleep. He is beside the fishers in their small craft, scratching the sea with their nets, to irritate it into yielding a small portion of the harvest that means life or death to their communities. And he is there directing his camera's eye to the townships, studded with crofts: they static while their inhabitants go through the turbulent processes of birth, growth, marriage and death.

It is extremely doubtful if a novelist of the likes and stature of Neil Gunn will ever again be produced by the Highlands. He was of his own time and he served with the utmost fidelity the needs of the Highland communities which were then crying out for the sympathetic, socially-conscious writer to express what they themselves could not do: plea for recognition in a national and comprehensive scheme of things. This is not to say that the need is less great at the present time, but to say that Neil Gunn, were he performing the function of a Highland propagandist today, would have to become more of a documentary novelist to the great loss to the growing corpus of Scottish literature. As it is, a novelist of his time, he presented his Highlands and his Highlanders in a way which pointed to the needs of Highland communities and which also added to the stature and status of Scotland's literature, to justify

Kurt Wittig's claim: 'Modern Scottish fiction reaches its highest peak in the novels of Neil M. Gunn'; and to fulfill the prophecy of Hugh MacDiarmid that Neil Gunn was likely to 'take rank as the foremost of living Scottish writers'.

Gunn's novels and short stories contain many things for many people, not only to Highlanders who may have become hazy about their origins, but to those others who have yet to acknowledge in their own due time that the Highlands and Islands of Scotland still retain the pervading atmosphere of an old significant culture which is even yet making its contribution to the world of Man's literary endeavours and to the continuing development of philosophies about his physical state and psyche.

Dunbeath shore

NEIL M. GUNN   NOVELIST OF THE NORTH

J. B. Caird

It has been said of Neil Gunn, almost as if it were a term of reproach, that he is a "regional novelist". "Regional" need not necessarily be a term of contempt - a regional writer can also be universal in his treatment of his theme and in his appeal, as Hardy and Mistral have shown. In some respects, one of the most cosmopolitan of all writers, James Joyce, was a regional novelist, since all his work, from "Dubliners" to "Finnegan's Wake", is concerned with the city of Dublin and the lives of its inhabitants. Indeed for Joyce Dublin was a microcosm of the universe. He said on one occasion, "If I can get to the heart of Dublin, I can get to the heart of all the cities in the world: in the particular is contained the universal". And so of Gunn: he has not limited himself as a novelist by confining his attention to the Northern Highlands, to the existences of crofters and fishermen. In their lives, as in those of Wordsworth's dalesmen, are to be found as much comedy and tragedy, gaiety and sorrow, as in the lives of any other community.

Not that he excludes the city, although his heart is not in it. In more than one of the novels - notably in Wild Geese Overhead and Drinking Well a significant part of the action takes place in the city. But even Edinburgh in The Drinking Well is a force that tends to deflect the hero from his real purpose. It is something alien and corrupting, to be avoided or escaped from at all costs. In The Drinking Well there is a very marked contrast between the austere splendour and simplicity of the north and the twisted complexity of the city. Alien alike to Iain Cattanach were the genteel primness of legal society and the rank soggy corruption in the closes of the old town. The contrast is strengthened in a way characteristic of Gunn - in his emphasis on food - on the homely excellence of the bannocks and butter of Iain's native community and on the tainted eggs served by his skimping Edinburgh landlady. In Highland River, too, there is an episode set in Glasgow, which is described as "a trap of nightmare - set within the cage-trap of the black tenements" - he conveys a vision of "sub-human life scurrying through putrefying smells".

In this aversion from the city he resembles another modern Scottish novelist, Fionn MacColla, in whose novel, "The Albannach" Glasgow plays a similar role. We are reminded too, of the attitude of yet another twentieth century Scottish writer who, like Gunn, is one of the most sensitive and subtle writers of his generation. I am referring to the Orcadian, Edwin Muir, whose most characteristic work has an incomparable sageness and serenity. In his "Autobiography", and also in some of his poems, he contrasts the idyllic simplicity and "piety" - I use the word in a non-denominational sense - of the Orkney of his childhood with the oppressiveness and, to him, grim, soul-destroying ugliness of life in Glasgow. In many of his poems Muir is striving to recreate a vision of the Garden of Eden, of man's primal innocence before the fall, of which he had intimations in Orkney as a child. There is a similar feeling although not quite so clear-cut, in Gunn. The pilgrimage of the hero in Highland River, for instance, in tracing the stream to its source, is an indication. It was "A thrilling exploration into the source of the river and the source of himself". He is, too, in more than one of his novels, attempting to trace the sources of the life of the people to their origins in the dawn of time. He does this more directly in Sun Circle, and indirectly in such works as The Silver Bough. He says at one point, "It is a far cry from the golden age, to the blue smoke of the heath fire and the scent of the primrose. Our river took a wrong turning somewhere! But we haven't forgotten the source."

For Gunn, as for Wordsworth (who referred to "Sorrow barricadoed evermore within the walls of cities") truth and spiritual health are not to be found in towns but rather away from the busy haunts of men, by the seashore, or by tracing a stream to its ultimate source on a lonely moorland, in a world of light and rock and dark sparse vegetation. He is, and in this respect he is unlike the majority of modern novelists, obsessed by purity - by purity of soul, by the purity of a clean northern landscape, by the purity of fresh uncontaminated water (notably in The Well at the World's End), or of whisky distilled in a pot still. In this connection we should not forget that Gunn has written the most eloquent of all treatises on the national drink, Whisky and Scotland.

He is fascinated, for instance, by what he calls the "innocence" of the scent of the primrose:- "the innocency of dawn on a strath on a far back morning of creation", and, talking about the Caithness landscape, he says "there was a purity about it all, stainless as the gull's plumage, wild and cold as its eye". Indeed he claims that the scent of the primrose and the glow of the heath fire vouchsafe him "visions" of "the golden age" of history, visions not dissimilar to Lewis Grassic Gibbon's evocations of the prehistoric hunters.

Yet once more Wordsworth comes to mind, the Wordsworth who condemned the materialistic Peter Bell in the following verse -

"A primrose by the river brim

A yellow primrose was to him
And it was nothing more."

To Gunn, as to Wordsworth, it was a good deal more. For him the primrose is intermediate between a catalyst like the "madeleine" in Proust's "A La Recherche du Temps Perdu", and a pure symbol. In Wild Geese Overhead, the birds are a symbol of liberation, and, over and over again, in The Green Isle of the Great Deep for instance, and in Highland River, he makes use of the nuts of the hazel of wisdom which are swallowed by the salmon of knowledge. Gunn himself has said, "nothing profound is ever finally and materially clear, but only glimpsed in its symbols".

An equally fruitful approach is his attitude towards the past of his country. An important feature in Gunn's novels is his attitude towards history. For him history is not an affair of kings and statesmen, of dynasties and political forces. To him these are merely froth. The essential is the life of the community, from prehistoric times onwards. It is significant that he stresses, not the differences between people belonging to different eras, but their similarities, both in physical appearance and in mental attitudes and emotional reactions. Over and over again he stresses this kinship. He emphasises those moments in our lives when we feel most in touch with our remote ancestors.

In Highland River, for instance, he is describing his hero's birthplace.

"On one side of the harbour mouth the place-name was Gaelic, on the other side it was Norse. Where the lower valley broadened out to flat fertile land the name was Norse, but the braes behind it were Gaelic. A mile up the river where the main stream was joined by its first real tributary, the promontory overlooking the meeting of the waters was crowned by the ruins of a broch that must have been the principal stronghold of the glen when the Picts, or perhaps some earlier people, were in their heydey. And all these elements of race still existed, along the banks of the river, not only visibly in the appearance of the folk themselves, but invisibly in the stones and earth. The "influence" continued sometimes so subtly that Ken had more than once been surprised into a quick heart-beat by the very stillness of certain ancient spots as though the spots had absorbed in some mysterious way not only the thought but the very being of the dark men of pre-history". These influences, he says, give one "moments of exquisite panic, of sheer delight".

Let us consider one or two points raised in this passage. The Norse element is equated with the sea, the indigenous Pictish element with the land. The two themes, the land and the sea, correspond to the outgoing and in-going facets of Gunn's personality. In writing about the sea, and what is connected with it, as in The Silver Darlings, he is objective, and dramatic, a chronicler of bold action and determination. When describing the land he is meditative, indrawn and poetic, a subtle and elusive interpreter of delicate intuitions - essentially a lyric poet. In a vivid phrase he describes a landscape as "a mover of the heart".

In that re-creation of ninth-century life in the area, Sun Circle, the two aspects appear to be almost deliberately juxtaposed - the rough, daring ruthlessness of a landward race, torn between the paganism of the old earth-worship and the appeal of a new Christian creed that enjoined humility and forgiveness.

It is perhaps, significant that, wherever in Gunn's novels the relationship between land and sea is one of conflict, as in Morning Tide and, to a certain extent, The Silver Darlings, it is always the women who are opposed to the sea, which they fear, distrust, and regard almost as a rival for their husbands' allegiance. Consciously or unconsciously, Gunn equates the poetry of the earth with the feminine principle, an equation not unrelated to the ancient worship of the earth mother. This passage, from Morning Tide suggests something of the sort.

"Silence and remoteness and peril. The vast night world of the moor. The high dark sky. Threading it to the river and the poaching of salmon. The half moon wanly tilted over and sinking. Every sense in the boy grew so alert that shapes and instincts crept out of his blood. An occult ecstasy revived the dark hollow of his fear with fire. He was being born to the earth, to the mother that is behind all mothers, as the sea, the father, is behind all fathers."

It is, perhaps, not entirely irrelevant to remind ourselves that Pictish society appears to have been matriarchal and that, basically, the people of the north-eastern Highlands are Pictish, with an imposition both of later Gaelic and of Norse elements. How far the early Pictish substratum was composed of people who had been in the land since neolithic times we do not exactly know. It is, at any rate, fascinating to find so eminent an authority as Professor Kenneth Jackson in his brilliant essay on "The Pictish Language", stating that it is not improbable that there were pre-Indo-European, i.e., pre-Celtic elements in the language spoken by the Picts. Here and there in his novels, Gunn, in his penetrating way, suggests atavistic influences of this kind. In The Silver Bough, which is avowedly archaeological in theme, the following dialogue occurs between Grant, the archaeologist, and Martin, the Landowner. They have been discussing the lives of the people who erected the cairn and stone circle.

"We know little enough about how or what they believed and then mostly from foreign sources. You might as well say that people were silent in their ceremonies at your cairn in Clachar because we do not know the tongue they spoke."

"Wasn't it some kind of Celtic tongue?"

"The neolithic people did not speak even any kind of Aryan tongue, much less a specific Celtic. It was an archaic tongue of which we know nothing."

"And it died with them?"

"No. It just died, but not with them. They took the invader's tongue, perhaps Pictish: but they lived on."

"I thought we didn't know much about the Picts' language."

"Neither we do, because there were more invaders and a new tongue called Gaelic, and you, who are still neolithic in your bones, literally your bones, actually speak yet another invader's language called English."

"The bones remain, but the languages die?"

"More than the bone remains."

"And how are you so sure about my bones?"

"Because to be sure is part of my business as an archaeologist. I see the bone of your skull as I see the bones in your ankles."

"And all this amounts to - what?"

"To knowledge," and Grant lifted his glass and drank. "

One of the occasions when we feel nearest to our prehistoric ancestors is when we are engaged in the chase: hence, perhaps, as Mr. Stewart Angus has pointed out, the importance played in Gunn's work by such activities as hunting and fishing. He is drawing too, upon vivid memories of boyhood, that period when we have most in common with our food-gathering and hunting forbears. Over and over again in the novels we encounter descriptions of wrestling with mighty salmon in native pools. He is also particularly successful in conveying the sensations of a boy or man when alone at night in a dark wood or on a desolate moor - another occasion on which we are close to the "primitive". He is a believer in what Jung has described as "the collective unconscious", what Yeats refers to as "The Great Memory" - the memory of the race itself.

The sense of community pervades all his novels, whether they are set in the ninth, nineteenth or twentieth centuries. But it is a community of independent individuals, not a community of mindless insects as The Green Isle of the Great Deep emphasises. In this, too, he resembles Wordsworth. The independent life of the dalesmen in Wordsworth's Cumberland was, in some respects, not unlike that of the crofter-fishing community from which Gunn sprang. They cherished similar ethical values, clung to the same splendid simplicities.

This sense of community, with its attendant virtues of frankness, hospitality and trust which flourished in the straths and glens of the Highlands, was broken by the Clearances, but established once more on a different footing in the crofting and fishing communities of the seaboard. Later it was broken once again by emigration and various economic factors.

Now this, briefly, is the theme of many of Gunn's novels. It is the theme of Butcher's Broom, The Silver Darlings, and The Grey Coast.

In Butcher's Broom, in a leisurely and elaborate way he attempts to recreate the life of the people in a Sutherland strath before they were struck by the terrible trauma of the Clearances. He describes not only the physical circumstances, the economy of their lives, the houses the lived in, the food they ate, the way they farmed their land and looked after their livestock, but also their way of life in a wider sense, the songs, verses and dances that gave gaiety and colour to their evenings, their very way of speech. Of their language, he remarks, "A man or woman might say in greeting 'It's the fine day that's in it,' as though he were setting the day in the hollow of the world so that they might with courteous detachment regard it." Of their songs he says:

"Now she sang a song he knew, an ancient song of love forsaken, in the music that was not only music to him but all the impulses and longings of his immemorial race caught for an immortal moment in body an brain. The sheer unconditional nature of this music has nothing to do with thought or intellect but only with absolutes like beauty or terror. They are apprehended in the blood and in the bowels, and the soul gives them light or fragrance, or the blindness of night."

Elsewhere in The Silver Darlings he refers to the effect of such musi in making the skin "run cold". He says that the song "was evolving itsel effortlessly out of a memory so old that it was quiet with contemplation He talks about "the awful, inexorable simplicity of the singing."

Gunn, though he writes in prose, is essentially a poet, with a poetic vision of the world and with a poet's sensitiveness, delicacy and, above all, precision in expressing it.

He describes the traditional observances, beliefs and superstitions of the people, the way they felt towards each other as members of a close knit community, their deep instinctive feelings for the strath itself, for its waters and hill-slopes where they and their forebears had dwelt for centuries. It is a picture of innocence and, like most forms of innocen it was betrayed. The very spiritual roots from which their civilisation drew its sustenance were poisoned: the ancient duty of hospitality to th needy and the homeless was proscribed.

It is interesting to observe that, although in Butcher's Broom Gunn is concerned with the Clearances, he is not at all melodramatic in his approach. The theme readily lends itself to the sensational - callous cruelty, eviction, the harrying and persecution of helpless, harmless people. The major part of Butcher's Broom is, however, not concerned with the physical processes of the Clearances themselves, but, as I have indicated, with the way of life of the people before they took place, with a distinctive and priceless civilisation that was destroyed. Gunn is essentially positive in his values. Understanding and irony rather than indignation mark his treatment of the theme.

In the opening of The Silver Darlings, Gunn describes succinctly the transition between the Clearances and the foundation of the fishing industry on the North-East coast of the Moray Firth. "The first year had been the worst. Many had died. Many had been carried away in empty lime ships. A great number had perished on the sea. But a greater number, it was believed, were alive in Nova Scotia and elsewhere in Canada and other lands, though fighting against dreadful tribulations and adversities. It had been a bitter and terrible time. Some said it had been brought upon them for their sins, and some said it had been a visitation of the Lord upon the world because of the wicked doings of the anti-Christ, Napoleon. But with Napoleon at last in St. Helena, the burnings and evictions went on; and as for their sins, to many of them, if not to all, it seemed that their lives had been pleasant and inoffensive in their loved inland valleys; and even in an odd year, when harvests had been bad and cattle lean, even now the memory of it seemed lapped around with an increased kindliness of one to another." This novel is more objective in its approach than most of the others, and this is in keeping with its theme. As in Butcher's Broom, he is dealing with a community, although here, too, as is demanded by the novel form, the main events are seen through the eyes of, and impinge on the lives of a few selected individuals. But, whereas Butcher's Broom is a chronicle of sadness and oppression, a bitter elegy, The Silver Darlings reflects a period of expansion and hope. One might well apply the titles of two of André Malraux's novels to characterize the two works, "Jours de Mépris" ("Days of Contempt") and "L'Espoir" ("Days of Hope"). It is painted on a much wider canvas than Butcher's Broom - indeed it is panoramic in its sweep. The difference between them reflects the difference between the settings of the two novels - the sheltered, enclosed nature of the fertile strath with its traditional way of life, and the illimitable open sea, bountiful yet undependable, to which the men driven out by the Clearances were tied by no traditional bonds. To them it was something new, exciting, dangerous and challenging, with a feeling about it of "glad, confident morning". For the sea, incompletely described by Arnold as "estranging", joins as well as severs. It marks the road to the ends of the earth, to adventure in strange places, and truly The Silver Darlings is a work heroic in scale and in character. We need only think of the chapter "Storm and Precipice" with its description of a voyage in a small boat through the Pentland Firth out into the open Atlantic, of the superb account of Finn's climbing the cliff in the Flannan Isles, of the enthralling shipwreck and rescue off the cliffs at Dunster. Other memorable, although less obviously dramatic episodes in the novel are the descriptions of the great cholera epidemic of 1832 and of the Revivalist mission meeting in Lewis, when the thwarted emotional life of the oppressed people finds expression. Together the two novels constitute a kind of prose epic of the north-eastern Highlands.

It should, however, be pointed out in passing that the development of the fishing industry was only a partial and temporary solution of the problem caused by the Clearances. I need hardly mention the drift southwards to the cities, the large-scale emigration overseas, and, of course, the evictions themselves were to continue for many a long year after some of the folk from Kildonan and Strathnaver came down to the sea coast. Indeed they were not to stop until the 1850s.

Later there came a time when the fishing industry itself went into decline and this is reflected in the earliest of Gunn's novels to be published, The Grey Coast, where the elegiac note is struck very strongly. Just compare the following two passages, the one from The Silver Darlings, describing the fishing industry in its flourishing days, and the other from The Grey Coast, depicting it in its twentieth-century decline.

"In the morning a woman would cry to man or boy, 'Are the boats in? or 'What luck to-day?' The questions flew over the land. When the boats were well-fished, hearts were uplifted and the daily tasks accomplished with cheerfulness and spirit. Figures could be seen moving here and there, up the braes, along the paths, dangling a string of herring. There was work for everyone. Along the road from Wick, carriers brought goods at all hours. Crofts would be stocked; a new house built and, above all, orders placed for new boats, not only in the flourishing yards at Wick, but in many a creek along the coast.

In the evening, when scores of boats headed for the fishing grounds, men and women would marvel, looking on that pretty scene, at the change that had come over their coast. No enchanter in the oldest legend had ever waved a more magical wand."

Now compare that with the following from The Grey Coast.

"And the fishing, at one time the great industry of the coast, was dying, visibly dying before the eyes of a single generation. Even in Ivor's childhood every little creek or fault in that dark precipitous sea-wall had been a hive of pulsing life. Good fishings and the land smiled, the shopkeepers throve, money flowed with a generous freedom . . . and now all that was past. The fishings were dwindling, boat hulks lay rotting at their haulage. The day of the sail and the small fishing creek was giving way before the ousting mastery of steam, the steam of the drifter and the railway . . . the wealth of communal life that had enriched the bleak seaboard with a rare self-sufficiency was growing thin in the blood and cold, was dying without hope."

These quotations prove that Gunn is not, as some people have suggested, an escapist novelist, basking in the fading splendour of a Celtic twilight, drugging himself with dreams of Tir nan Og. He sees and understands grim economic realities, although he is not obsessed by them. And, as with the sea, so with the land. He can evoke a landscape with rare sensitiveness and beauty, and can penetrate to the meaning behind it. He can describe a storm on land with as great dramatic power as he can a storm at sea, as witness the snowstorm in The Drinking Well, one of the most memorable of its kind in Scots fiction, fit to be classed with the storm that raged over the Mounth in "Sunset Song" or the storm in "The House with the Green Shutters".

So far we have considered Gunn as a historical novelist, as the interpreter, in fiction, of the north-eastern Highlands of Scotland. But, of course, he is much more than that. He has a highly individual vision of life, a vision which is, perhaps, most fully communicated in those two more personal novels, Morning Tide and Highland River, both set obviously in the author's native Dunbeath. The story of Morning Tide has a surface simplicity that is disarming - a ship coming home through heavy seas at dawn - a young girl's first love affair - a poaching expedition. But its importance lies in the human values it embodies - the sense of community, the strength of family life. In its account of a boy's reactions to his environment, and of his emotional development, it is an example of a "Bildungs Roman", a novel of "apprenticeship", of the growth to maturity, like Joyce's "Portrait of the Artist" or Thomas Mann's "Tonio Kröger".

Highland River is, along with Edwin Muir's "Autobiography", one of the finest accounts I know of the development of a poetic mind from childhood to manhood. His theme is here essentially the unfolding of a personality, moulded by the influences of sea, cliffs, moors and river - essentially a Wordsworthian conception, an extremely beautiful, sensitive, poetic work; in his own words, "a thrilling exploration into the source of the river and the source of himself."

In Highland River, Gunn flashes back from the present, the mature

Kenn, to his boyhood in the distant past, thence to the middle past, and back again to the present, - a series of shifting perspectives in time, and he also gives us the impression of the illusoriness of time. Kenn, the boy, Kenn, the adolescent, and Kenn, the mature man, are all one: they appear to co-exist. This principle of co-existence applies, for Gunn, to the race as well as the individual. The Pict, the broch-builder of the Dark Ages, is one with the crofter-fisherman who now dwells in the strath.

Now finally which other novelists does Gunn most closely resemble? Which novelists appear to have influenced him most? Many years ago Hugh McDiarmid once remarked to me that Gunn did not begin writing in the manner we consider to be characteristic of him until he read Joyce and Proust. There may be some truth in this. I have already compared Gunn's use of the primrose to Proust's use of the "madeleine" the small cake whose taste recalled the whole world of his childhood at Combray. He resembles Proust, too, in his delicate renderings of sense impressions shading off into something that is beyond the senses. Although Gunn's themes are poles apart from Proust's, I can think of no other novelist writing in English whose mode of perception so closely resembles his.

In his use of the stream of consciousness technique and in his emphasis on epiphanies - those rare moments of intense insight that appear to give significance to life, he may have been influenced by Joyce. In The Well at the World's End he talks about "those moments of penetration, the instant when they went through the boundary, the moment when they saw the crystal water in the well".

He resembles Lawrence in his evocation of the unconscious, in his description of the subtle relationships between man and nature, and between man and the animal kingdom. Like Lawrence, too, he is greatly concerned with the primitive, with what links us to our remote ancestors of palaeolithic and neolithic times. In Sun Circle, for example, he appears in his recreation of primitive life, to have been influenced, to his detriment perhaps, by the Lawrence of "The Plumed Serpent", the Lawrence who deified the dark impulses of the blood and exalted strange gods. The following passage, not really typical of Gunn, illustrates the point: "She drew up at a yard or two, and stood quite still. The mother looked at her back and her eyes grew narrow and full of deadly intimacy. The girl turned round. Complete woman knowledge went between them."

He resembles Conrad in his obsession by the sea and in his remarkable descriptions of storms, as in Morning Tide and The Silver Darlings. He resembles him, too, in his emphasis on elemental qualities that make civilisation possible - courage, physical and moral, endurance, truth and sincerity, and, above all, loyalty. For Gunn, as for Conrad, betrayal is the ultimate crime.

But on the whole I should say that these writers were the midwives to his artistic progeny, rather than its grandparents. They may have helped him to evolve, to find his feet sooner than he would have done otherwise. He is no mere imitator of other men's themes and styles. He has a vision of his own, a vision of the Highlands and of the whole of human life - and a voice of his own. Of him it might well be said, as it was said of Yeats - "he gave a tongue to the seacliffs" - aye, and to more than the seacliffs - to the brown rolling moors with their lochans as well, to the desolate straths to which he has restored something of their ancient music, and to the chameleon-like and subtle loveliness of the ancient province of Cat.

The Dun, Dunbeath

BEYOND HISTORY AND TRAGEDY
NEIL GUNN'S EARLY FICTION

Francis Russell Hart

For me, Neil Gunn's twenty novels are the finest body of work as ye
produced by a Scottish novelist. To envision a transcendence of high
comedy in the face of the history and tragedy of Highland experience i
the gist of his achievement. First came The Grey Coast (1926) and la
(unless he changes his mind) The Other Landscape (1954). The titles
suggest, perhaps misleadingly, a dominant concern with Highland plac
we can watch this concern emerge and change in a consideration of thr
wide-spaced novels: The Grey Coast (1926), The Lost Glen (1932), an
Second Sight (1940). But perhaps the more central perception in Gunn
is not of place but of time, and it belongs often to the innocent eye of t
child, which turns our attention to novels of Highland boyhood: Mornin
Tide (1930), Highland River (1937), and Young Art and Old Hector (19
and by extension to Highland "growing up" The Serpent (1943) and The
Drinking Well (1946). But the perception of Highland time is collectiv
as well as personal, and he has written three ambitious "historical"
novels, all about the inadequacy of history as a way of seeing: Sun
Circle (1933), Butcher's Broom (1934), and The Silver Darlings (1941
During the Second World War, with the mythic dystopia The Green Isl
of the Great Deep (1944), there seems to occur in Gunn's fiction an ex
pansion and displacement of theme into urgencies of the mid-20th Cent
ury world. They are, of course, anticipated in earlier novels such as
Wild Geese Overhead (1939). But that is a story to be saved for anoth
er time. And for many of his admirers, the earlier books remain the
favourites. Without drawing any hard and fast chronological or develo
mental line - and including The Drinking Well while I omit Wild Geese
Overhead, I will speak here of the "early fiction" and its several effor
to offer a vision beyond the history and tragedy of the modern Highlanc
We begin with the immediate landscape. The Grey Coast (1926), Th
Lost Glen (1932), and Second Sight (1940) all depict the contemporary
Highlands as a place of severe economic depression, of depopulation,
the social decay and bitterness attendant on the fading of old life-givin
rhythms. The Lost Glen, the bitterest, sums up best:

> "The Land was too old. Scarred and silent, it was settling down
> into decay. The burden of its story had become too great to
> carry. . . It was not that the spirit was dead but that it had passe

There was no longer any meaning in living there. How terrible, how awful, the slow movement of time, with its grey sterile land! . . . He hid his mind in what had been friendly and fresh and full of labour and leisure and happiness; the old music, the games, the fierce passions, the fights, the stir, the excitement, the loneliness, the grey mists, the sun, the sea; life centred on itself, young life fierce or glowing or dreamy, but life, with belief in its time and place."

All three novels focus intensively on intricately conceived character groupings in roles that are at once culturally representative and primordial. All are in various states of silent, but urgent spiritual conflict, each relationship a power struggle for selfhood and mastery. All three are plotted on murders, accidental violences, or triumphant self-destructions, provoked by sexual threat, socio-economic conflict, and ideological warfare; the three in Gunn are closely interrelated.

The conflicts take several forms. In Grey Coast there are four characters: Maggie, niece and housekeeper on the croft of her uncle "ould Jeems," is loved quietly and hopelessly by young and poor and desperate fisherman Ivor Cormack, and lusted brutally after by Tait of Tullach Farm, a destructive despot of a small landowner who maintains his power by helping keep up Jeem's poor croft, not knowing that Jeems, sly old sailor, has gold hidden. The plot is the silent, tense evolution of these relationships in the course of the intensely rendered little domestic rhythms of the hard croft life. The technical achievement is the dramatization of Maggie's consciousness. But the focus of triumphant meaning is on Jeems: slyly he plays with Tullach; obliquely he pimps for his unwilling niece; defiantly he poaches on Tullach's land; climactically he sides with youth against lustful middle-aged avarice, willing his gold to Maggie and robbing Tullach of his power.

The conflict between Jeems and Tullach is a subtle, slow Highland contest of words and wits, primordially suited to the grey coast of Caithness. Tullach's lusts are of the earth, while Jeems' defiant whimsies are of the sea, and old sailor taunts land-bound farmer with erotic reminiscences of foreign ports. This is the place where sea and land greyly meet in "fierce mating of sea and cliff." Place and its conflict are eternal. The characters come at last to a distanced vision of themselves as archaic figures of legend, even as they remain fully psychologized on a naturalistic landscape, two young lovers and their aged satyr of a collaborator fighting sullenly for a little life against the timeless life-denying forces of the Tullachs.

Such struggles culminate in Gunn's novels in moments of vision at once atavistic and portentous. The landscape, local and particular in

configuration, acts reciprocally with the growth of inward vision to pro
duce such moments. The mind "of its own inscrutable volition pursues
hidden ways of dream and thought" far beneath the grey surfaces of dail
croft life. "And of all places, such a grey strip of crofting coast, flank-
ed seaward by great cliffs, cliffs 'flawed' as in a half-sardonic humour
of their Creator to permit of the fishing creek, was surely of this dual-
ity of the mind, whereby the colourless, normal life becomes at once a
record of the stolidly obvious and of the dream-like unknown." Here is
the genesis of that "other landscape" on which, throughout Gunn's fiction
essential human roles and actions are played out.

Lost Glen is less successful. But the conflict is similar: a fusion of
sexual rivalry, a social struggle for integrity and mastery, an ideological conflict. The destructive menace is Colonel Hicks, retired
Indian soldier, hunting and living where he can luxuriate in power on a
small income, sadistically probing the lazy deviousness of the locals.
His compassionate, romantic niece sees in him what is to become
Gunn's essential vision of evil: a shadow

> "coming between one and the sweet freedom of life . . . tinging
> things, taunting them, in spite of oneself. It was bigger than
> that; in some way it transcended the personal altogether; as if
> it were not merely her uncle's mind, but an altogether bigger
> mind, the mind of a world . . . One wanted to escape from it,
> to get out of its condition of mind, so that tne freed eyes might
> look on the silver and golden apples in their purity, and then
> look downward at the ancient necromantic earth, look long and
> nakedly, and penetrate to where the antique stirred bronze
> shapes in a fluid darkness."

The ultimate response to such a shadow will be the reaffirmation of
archaic comedy; but only bitter, destructive irony seems available to
the young gillie Ewen. Disgraced as a student, responsible on his return for his father's drowning, and now fading into "this bloody menial
service" of the gillie, Ewen has replaced his earlier spiritual ardour
with a "terrible and blasting irony." Yet, along with the dangerous
luxury of despair, there is in him the lovable folly of a Lord Jim determined not to flee. Ewen is melodramatically the hero as tragic young,
Gael, yet his ironic honesty tells him as much. He sees "that the
Colonel and himself were chance figures in a drama that affected the
very earth under his feet. Being chance figures, they did not matter;
were indeed figures of melodrama. But none the less did the earth
await the outcome of their secret strife, as if they stood for an ultimate
conquest or defeat." The arrogant, hysterical colonel tries brutally to
rape the crofter's daughter Ewen loves. Ewen procrastinates like Ham

let. He resolves not to murder, but accident leads to a dark, remote confrontation; and having throttled the colonel and tumbled him over a cliff, he sets forth to his own death at the scene of his father's drowning. What has been lost?

The "lost glen" of the title, a pibroch by Ewen's friend, commemorates the myth of a glen "innocent of human being," and for Ewen it is the lost locus of innocence which "the leaders of humanity had all searched for." Is it not then, the "lost glen" of Ewen's people? The book's integrity hinges on the relation of these "losses" to two kinds of innocence: one glen known always in vision, the other in "time and place" on this "old land" now given over to "the degradation of poverty in a world where money was the supreme power."

This is 1932. By 1940 with Second Sight, the locale is the same, but the terms of the struggle have been redefined. The browbeaten gillie is the victim of a hunting vacationer whose arrogance is intellectual, whose destructiveness is a will to "analyse" and invalidate all such archaic modes of experience as "Second Sight." Meanwhile, the hunter's fellow sophisticate and spiritual adversary Harry, with whom he competes for the killing of the great legendary deer King Brude, is acquiring his own form of "second sight", "as if the scales had come off your eyes." As one antagonist self-destructively loses himself, the other finds himself in a renewal of vision, finds the true, unsentimentalised value in local life, and finds love. The coming of vision and love is a freeing of the true self - Gunn would later call it the Second Self - from all the forces of modern intelligence that menace it. The climax for Harry is a moment of vision on the mountain top when the mist lifts; for Helen it is a moment of identity with the hunted beast; for Geoffrey, the destroyer, it is a moment when the brutal triumph of the destructive hunter over the heart of this place turns into self-disintegration.

Second Sight introduces the linked themes and motifs of Gunn's later fiction: the imperative of renewed vision, the translation of traditional superstition into an experience of self-transcendence (second self in second sight). Place has become the "other landscape" of the hunt, where ethic and ceremony of hunter and hunted are eternal, and where the hunt is personal and sexual as well as social and cultural. Evil, unchanged in its primordial character, is incarnate in the pseudo-scientism of analytic intelligence, destructive and self-destructive. The working out of self-destructive evil is plotted superficially on the level of popular mystery-violence. The protagonist is urbane and sophisticated and in need of a restorative retrogression, an atavistic withdrawal, into the archaism of boyhood or "primitive" vision.

The plausible characterization of the boy-visionary himself is difficult. But the three early novels of visionary boys remain for many readers Gunn's most admired: <u>Morning Tide</u> (1930), <u>Highland River</u>, (1937), and <u>Young Art and Old Hector</u> (1942). Hugh, Kenn and Art are as different as the books they dominate. But all are shy, loyal, fierce proud, defiant in their instinct for freedom and self-preservation, secretive, violently adventurous, and intensely aware of places and per sons in their immediate surroundings. <u>Morning Tide</u> is a massively impressionistic, conventionally ordered account of "the boy's" proud and loving discoveries of this world of archetypal domesticities and the elemental rivalries between them: red sister and dark sister, men and women ("like a group caught in a grey dawn of history, or legend, their separateness from the men fateful and eternal"), his mother the earth and his father the sea. The first of three parts is his discovery of his father, the fishing captain, climaxing with the storm and his father's triumph of seamanship. The second is his struggle with the mystery a the loving repression of his mother, ending in the tragic economic nec essity of his brother's departure. In the third, with his father away an his brother gone, with his sisters in sexual danger and his mother dang erously ill, he learns the power and exhilaration of his own manhood, t inevitabilities of fear and flight and death. In each he is "the boy's eye opening in wonder, and the boy's passions in response, concrete and archetypal, instinctively delicate. "All that had happened throughout th evening flashed through Hugh's mind, not so much in vivid images as in a vivid impressionism." His essential response is not gloomy intro-spection, but rather the ecstasy that breaks upon moments of sheer un-reflective delight. The three parts have the same ending: a joy in the triumphant courage of life consummated by the urge to be "off and away

"Hugh ran. Tears were streaming down his face . . . O red ecstasy of the dawn! . . .

A flush of happiness bathed his heart. His head turned quick as a hawk's. He started running . . .

Unless he went to the woods - for an offering? His head turned. And all at once he started running, his body light and fleet, his bare legs twinkling across the field of the dawn . . ."

The boy Kenn of <u>Highland River</u> is differently individualized. The man Kenn, mathematician, physicist, wounded and gassed veteran of the First World War, is central. The boy is locus of remembered ex-periences and archetypal drives whose lasting significance the man sets out to discover. Place and time are indistinguishable from those of <u>Morning Tide</u>, but very different kinds of hero and pattern make for different symbolic localities. The "morning tide" is the first timeless phase in the boy's awakening self-consciousness, in a pattern of daily time without historic locality. Archetypal and individual remain so close that the locality of place is self-transcendent. Kenn's "highland river" is from the outset of the quest explicitly archetypal: the book's topic - its objective as exploratory autobiography - is the problem of the relation between specific boy and specific river, which has somehow produced the ground of the man's entire experience, indestructible "through his boyhood approaches," and carried over "to every other environment in life."

Individuality begins in a relation between person and original place that evolves so as to generate self-transcendence in both: the place reveals an "other landscape", the person discovers a "second self", and the two fuse, outer and inner worlds, in the renewal and transcendence of vision. No mystical vagueness is tolerated; precise knowledge complements the sense of wonder, as when Kenn looks at the salmon pool and <u>knows</u> that the epic capture of the fish <u>happened there</u>. The search moves always toward greater and greater explicitness: "Kenn has an urge to be explicit, even to labour what is infinitely elusive, because the farther he goes towards the source of his river the more he feels there is in this very elusiveness the significance he would like to hold." This urge gives the book its form, as difficult as <u>Morning Tide</u> is simple, or as <u>Young Art and Old Hector</u> is unpretentiously oblique.

The reconstructive intelligence is always in control of design, choosing and interweaving the immediacies of the boy with the later experience and reflections of student, scientist, and soldier. But the reconstructive intelligence is always conscious, too, of the pitfalls of its own symbolic imagination. The two worlds of person and past, person and place, boy and river, must interpenetrate without violating each other's integrity, as in the scrupulousness of Highland conversation: "Kenn is sensitive to false symbolism here . . . All that has happened is that in the acuteness of his vision the inessentials have faded out. The figure may be ageless, but it is a living figure to whom in time past his erratic emotions were directed: who once, in a bitter cold, took Kenn's hands and warmed them in his hair." The archetypalizing imagination is austerely precise, fixed in the sensory reality of the original apprehension, yet committed in retrospect to an image of essential significance. And as in <u>Grey Coast</u>, so here in <u>Highland River</u>, this habit of vision by which place and time are transcended is traced back to the place that produced it - for only back there is the "other landscape" to be found.

The transition from Kenn to <u>Young Art and Old Hector</u> is a shift of setting as well as a sharp change in mode and form to gnomic comedy and dramatic episode. The river is now a far away boundary between here and "the world beyond." The narrator simply presents scenes and sensation, while comments all come from wondrously devious and whimsically wise Old Hector. The method is as dramatic as the method of Highland River is meditative or the method of Morning Tide is impressionistic. The book began as a series of periodical sketches, freeing the author from more ambitious and restrictive structural ideas. The episodes centre on the relationship of a boy and a neighbour, a relationship beyond home and family; Art is initiated into a community, a human locale, rather than into a family or a natural setting. The transferral of a wisdom from Hector to Art becomes the definition of the place that has produced and preserved that wisdom. Each new stage of illumination is an immediate experience for the boy and an emblem of life for the old man; thus reality and myth are identified. The fitting climax comes when at long last Hector takes Art to the river.

Art has long been frustrated in his desire to visit that far-off "dark stranger of his dreams." When Hector, on his own farewell journey, takes him there, it is to discover that he must go home again, that he has his place, that in fact he is taking Hector's place: so ends the process of transferral and traditional inheritance which the book enacts. Here at the river the little world ends and the great one begins. The littleness of this world and its wisdom are now one, to be justified together as Art asks Hector whether he is sorry now, "at the end of the day," that he never left this place.

> "Well, if I had gone away, I wouldn't have been here walking with
> you, for one thing. And for another, I like to be here. You see,
> I know every corner of this land, every little burn and stream,
> and even the boulders in the stream. And I know the moors and
> every lochan on them. And I know the hills, and the passes, and
> the ruins, and I know of things that happened here on our land
> long long ago, and men who are long dead I knew, and women.
> I knew them all . . . It's not the size of the knowing that matters,
> I think," said Old Hector, "it's the kind of the knowing. If, when
> you know a thing, it warms your heart, then it's a friendly know-
> ing and worth the having."

The place is a small coastal crofting community "in the West"; the Clash nearby, now forbidden land, is the real place in the history of these people, but the Clearances ended that. Time and place are remarkably free of the important particulars and domestic solemnities that localise Morning Tide and Highland River. What matters is wisdom and wisdom is a gnomic, oblique, loving humour for which "nowhere" and "somewhere", "going" and "coming" are more than anything the counters of playful paradox. Art is a dramatic and enigmatic centre in the process of acquiring wisdom and place, growing into the heroic boy, the force of anarchic and defiant innocence, that he would become in The Green Isle of the Great Deep (1944). The later book is in some respects Gunn's most important, but the earlier has something more precious, and in the economy of its scenic form, the lucid understated quality of its style, and the profound simplicity of its comic vision, it is matchless among his books.

Before The Green Isle came The Serpent (1943) and not long after it The Drinking Well (1946), two ambitious extensions of Highland boyhood into autobiographical critiques of modern Highland culture and economy. Tom the Philosopher and Iain Cattanach are young men from Highland villages who go away, are educated into the world of early 20th Century social and intellectual history, and return, one a disgrace and the other a philosophical outcast. Each is a transformed youth come to review traditional Highland life at a certain moment in history - both stories are emphatically dated. Yet, as both titles suggest, each must somehow transcend his own somewhat superficial historicity in a return to archaic symbol or life-source.

The Serpent begins and ends with the death of its hero, "a death so startling that deep in the mind of the countryside the old menacing images would stir and lift their dark heads". The old man is off for a sunny climb up a hill near his village. His expanding retrospects are punctuated by climbs and rests, the method of Gibbon's trilogy. He is moving toward the height from which Ross-shire can be seen from sea to sea, with humans moving slowly at crofting tasks so as to give "the illusion of an inner meaning or design that never changed". He is climbing back to old ways exiled by the Clearances, to a locus and a view of the past which contradict his own radically progressive attitudes. Up on the vacant moor he rests in a state of blissful transcendence, an adder slips from the heather stalks, and he feels its touch and dies. A young shepherd finds him, picks him up, "Whereupon a serpent of monstrous length issued, as it seemed, out of the left arm, out of the very hand... The shepherd turned and ran, and in the first few steps he lived through those years of his youth, the impressionable years of prophecy and curse, with the Serpent that would devour the atheist who had killed his own father." Friendship reasserts itself; the "primal fear" is forgotten, and he "sees Tom home."

Two serpents have warred in Tom. He had been called back from the exhilarating scepticism of late Victorian Glasgow as a young man when his father was disabled. The conflict between them leads up to the violent confrontation in Tom's tool shop, his haven for local sceptics,

where the thundering elder denounces Tom for having delivered himsel
to the Serpent, and the dying father, the "grey face, the grey beard, th
blazing eyes . . . The power of the father created in the image of God
The tribal power, "lifts a staff to chastise his blasphemous son, and
pitches forward dead at the feet of one who will now be looked upon as
father-slayer.

The elder was partly right. The father-son conflict is so carefully,
movingly managed as to arouse a difficult division of feeling in the
reader. But he sees that Tom has delivered himself to a serpent, and
it will take another to free him. His sceptical modernity, presented
with the intellectual excitement Gunn himself felt as a youth in Edward
ian London and Edinburgh, has become a cunning destructiveness, a
serpent of wisdom, of a pagan primordial love of earth, is the counter
force. His intellectuality belongs to specific decades, and throughout
the narrative he is associated with clocks and clock-time. Yet his ass
iation with timeless tragedies of love and domestic conflict, and with
the warfare of the serpents, suggests the timelessness of his real
struggle.

Tom is a sceptic of the turn of the 20th Century. Iain Cattanach is t
young man _entre deux guerres_ arguing political and economic issues,
debating the future of the Highlands under nationalism or socialism or
enlightened landlordism. His return from the city, like Tom's, brings
on conflict with his father, carries him through an ordeal of personal
redemption, and ends in the same archaic love of the land that prevails
at Tom's death. The Drinking Well is not, for me, one of Gunn's best
books. It includes too much. It suffers from the same overabundance
of discursive argument and arbitrary symbolic design that characteriz
the huge ideological romance Compton Mackenzie had finished the year
before (1945). Yet it has splendid panoramas unmatched in better nove
the brawl in an Edinburgh law office, the drunken visionary night walk
the Royal Mile, the vivid experience of Iain's shepherding over a Gram
pian pass in an early spring snowstorm. Visions of city and visions of
pastoral land vie for reality. Iain's Edinburgh talk and adventures rev
to him the awful senselessness, brutality, and grandeur of Scottish his
tory. The city is history. The land of the sheep and the snow is non-
historic, and it is by love of the land that Iain is haunted and saved. T
title indicates the symbolic place where that love is renewed. The wel
of the "mad" old woman appears empty; yet the emptiness is only an
optical illusion - the well is never really dry. Such is the love of the
land.

If there are too many ideological symbols uneasily aggregated in a
heavily discursive narrative, the novel is the fullest text of Gunn's ide

of modern Highland history. It follows three ambitious earlier narratives, broadly historical and densely documented.

The modern historical novel of the Highlands could emerge only when the epic absurdity of Culloden had been displaced by the more comprehensive, domestic tragedy of the Clearances. But how is such a subject to be fictionalized? The tragedy, says Eric Linklater, "is indisputable, unrelieved, and irreparable; and because there is no profit in crying over spilt milk, irony is the way to deal with it." In their different ways, the most notable three modern attempts all transcend irony; and all three, as well, eschew the premises of the traditional historical novel, simply because history's lessons are too abstract and too devastating by themselves.

In "Consider the Lilies"(1968), Iain Crichton Smith says he is not "competent to do an historical study of the period, "but has done, rather, "a fictional study of one person, an old woman who is being evicted." The historicity of his subject is not so easily muted. If it doesn't matter, then Smith might have avoided the distractions of emphatic anachronism by not having historic antagonists argue the issues of the Clearances in the old woman's little croft house and in her bewildered presence.

But there it is. And inevitably one tries to understand history and old Mrs. Scott's personal tragedy together, and this means seeing her story as somehow in metaphoric or contrapuntal relation to the movement of "history." It is Donald MacLeod who interprets it. MacLeod "knew that his hatred was not simply for those who were bent on destroying the Highlands, not simply for the Patrick Sellars, but for the Patrick Sellars in the Highlanders, those interior Patrick Sellars with the faces of old Highlanders who evicted emotions and burnt down love." Against them the old woman stands at last, against threat and bribery, church and factor alike; she triumphs over the fearful waste, the emotional evictions, of her own past, and somehow (for Smith, though not perhaps for the reader) the particulars of history no longer matter much at the end.

Fionn MacColla's "And the Cock Crew" (1945) goes to an opposite extreme. From Smith's deliberate dramatic restriction it moves to cosmic conflicts of perspective and a central character of extraordinary spiritual power, capable of violent convulsions of vision, the conscientious minister who, like Peter, three times betrays his people as they await his leadership in resisting eviction. His betrayals are moments of self-doubt grounded in the egoism of one who sees sin everywhere. On the verge of the evictions he opens his Sabbath sermon prophesying forty years of wandering in the wilderness, and then collapses speechless and sobbing in his pulpit as his people leave in despair.

Prior to this final betrayal, literally in the dark night of the soul (set

carefully in the hellish flickering of the smithy), he has gone groping t
his defeated rival the old poet. Their dialogue is the long centre of thi
short book, and as Fearchar argues the historical necessity of resist-
ance and Zachairi counters with his own theological rationalization of
inaction, the book's scope as a parable of leadership, spiritual betray
and visionary conflict is evident. We have moved far indeed from the
dramatic simplicity of Iain Crichton Smith to a highly conceptualized
theological parable. How shall we locate the third novel, <u>Butcher's
Broom</u>?

Centred on the "same events" it is profoundly different from both.
The definer of genres would no doubt consider it the only "historical
novel" of the three, and "history" is part of its central issue. The essential conflict here is not between humanism and calvinism or between
poetry and theology, but between mythic and historic views of personal
ity and community; it is a conflict that will persist in the dialectic of
Gunn's novels. The title identifies a bitter and unfolding irony in the
clan badge of the Sutherland, the sign of a pre-feudal, matriarchal pro
tectorate turned into an emblem of brutal rejection. The enemy is
neither MacColla's genocidal England nor Smith's love-evicting creed:
Gunn could never satisfy himself with the epic chauvinism of the one,
and he is too compassionate an interpreter of presbyterian severity to
rest with the other. The enemy is the "improving" spirit of a perverte
clan matriarchy.

When the "improvers" came to clear Sutherland glens, they found the
young men away, in their chief's service in a foreign war, promised
land and homes on their return. The women, as from time immemoria
were left with helpless old men and children. This grim fact is framed
in Gunn's essentially matriarchal view of archaic community. What m
in his callous utilitarian rationalism calls "history" is really a legenda
continuity of "innumerable women whose suffering and endurance were
like little black knots holding the web of history together." It is a
central irony that the "chieftain" who betrays her people is a woman.
And suitably the novel is focused on a matriarchal counterpart to the
Bitch Countess, Dark Mairi, and the delicate central relationship is
between her and the deserted, unwed mother, Elie, whom in her place
on the moral outskirts of man's "lawful" community Mairi takes to live
with her and her grandson. Their domestic grouping, elemental, matriarchal, is the novel's central reality and the norm by which the entir
community is progressively seen and understood. "In the centre of thi
gloom was the fire, and sitting round it, their knees drawn together,
their heads stooped, were the old woman, like fate, the young woman,
like love, and the small boy with the swallow of life in his hand".

Dark Mairi is the tragic centre of Gunn's vision. But she cannot serve as a central consciousness like Smith's Mrs. Scott or a dominant interpretive perspective like MacColla's Zachairi. And this is one of the novel's problems. She is the epitome of the traditional wisdom and practicality menaced by history in the guise of the scientific arrogance of the "improvers," whose intellectual negation turns as it always must to physical violence. The arrogance and the violence must be fully drawn, and Gunn's novel must be much larger and fuller than Smith's vignette or MacColla's parable-dialogue. Mairi and Elie move in a community for whom Mairi represents a wise continuity with the past, an earthy tolerance beyond "moral" barriers, and a legendary pers- pective within which they can identify themselves. The "improvers" are destroyers; her place in the community is as its healer. Born by the sea she carries its specifics and simples back to her people in the glen. Her life and power are rooted in the local earth, and both are magical, amoral, and utterly practical ; she is no dreamy Celtic "primitive": "Where all is magic, only the utterly practical person like Mairi can use it, troubled neither by the self-consciousness of the sceptic nor the idealism of the poet". Exiled at last with her people, she wanders dazed to the glen and is destroyed with ritual brutality by the dogs of the shepherd who has displaced her people. The book's end is her death march. Yet her death affects the reader as her tragic leg- ends help to heal innumerable and nameless other women brutally wound- ed by male history. Thus, "by some still more profound alchemy, the very tragedy which ended Mairi's story gave to the possibility of tragedy in Elie's story the last strength of all." When Elie finds herself in the song of another bereaved and deserted girl, she is carrying life onwards, extending Mairi's alchemy, healing by virtue of "humanity's final logic, tragedy".

The novel's articulation obviously is far beyond the conscious under- standing of Mairi or her community. The interpretive narrator's vision must comprehend both Mairi's practical vision and the other "logics" by which men cut off from her archaic wisdom would rationalize its des- truction. Their pretensions to an illusory historical pattern called Progress must be seen analytically for what they really are: "That this progress has proved illusory merely destroys the name they gave to their excuse, and strips their lust for possession to its naked strength." The factor's murderous hatred is to be explained not in Smith's psycho- logical terms or MacColla's theological-political ones, but in terms of a myth of life itself: "when any man opposes the fundamental principle of life in another, he must, by the irksome consciousness or subcon- sciousness of what he is doing, become antagonistic and violent, and

will hunt about in the other's life for what he can despise and hate."
Violence always begins as spiritual violence directed against the vital
principle in another's life. The doomed community has life:

> "the hot blood, the old wisdom, the urge through music to the sting
> of love, the quick feet, the flash, the fire, the withdrawal, the
> black pain, the red eye, the restless eternal beat, beat, beat of
> the heart . . . (the) love of the land, love of its visible features
> as something near and natural to them as their own limbs . . .
> The sun, the wind, the shapes of things, the smells, the sound
> of their own voices, the singing, the laughter, the sorrow, the
> lore, the passion - all that centuries upon centuries had fashioned
> in man's or God's image . . ."

The evocation is strongly coloured, and some readers may find it
too general to be quite free of the sentimental, overwhelming local
realities with a vision of longing. But how else can he identify the
crises of human value in the ritual simplicities of such a life for an
audience presumably sophisticated by the "progressive" rationalisms
of the historic destroyers of that life? The risks are necessary. If
there is sentimentality, however, it is more likely in the oversophisti-
cation of the sense of "tragedy" and its rhetorical overemphasis. If
tragedy is to be the "last strength of all", tragedy is real enough in the
brute facts plainly perceived and stated by the old people of the community. Here, however, is a hint as to the book's uneasiness. Gunn's
own ultimate vision partakes of transcendent comedy; he could never
be easy with a view of "humanity's final logic" as "tragedy", for man's
essential drama is one of light not darkness, and his preservative
wisdom is delight.
Sun Circle (1933) and The Silver Darlings (1941) are free of the tragic
historical particularity of Butcher's Broom, and both end their rendition
of historic convulsions with affirmations of defiant humour.

> "For there is a secret here that neither the lovely dead nor the
> swift gods know. It is the immortality of life, the young heart
> against the mother heart, and its music sets a man brooding or
> walking in defiance, and the memory of it can in a lonely place
> make him shout with defiance and laugh, for he knows the chall-
> enge of his own creation against the immortality of the jealous
> gods."

The title Sun Circle might apply to both books. Deriving from an
archaic charm, it is for Gunn the principle of personal wholeness.
In the cataclysmic historical worlds of Sun Circle and The Silver Darlings, it is the lesson of survival:

"As the Sun put a circle round the earth and all that it contained, so a man by his vision put a circle round himself. At the centre of this circle his spirit sat, and at the centre of his spirit was a serenity for ever watchful. Sometimes the watchfulness gave an edged joy in holding at bay the demons and even the vengeful lesser gods, and sometimes it merged with the Sun's light into pure timeless joy."

To be divided within, to disintegrate in spirit, is to surrender to darkness - such is the advice learned in Sun Circle by the two rival leaders, Haakon the Viking and Aniel the Celt, from their older counsellors. The novel is so concerned throughout with the moral and political education of the young leaders that it is rich in long passages of instruction and hence perhaps the most quotable of Gunn's novels, the one in which a "life philosophy" is most fully expounded. It is philosophical romance rather than novel.

It was written at a time when numerous novelists, excited by new developments in primitive anthropology, experimented with archaic psychology in preChristian settings. The temptation to mingle imaginative psychology with a highly conceptualized "primitivism" is evident in most, and Sun Circle is no exception. It is for Gunn a unique opportunity to prophesy an idea of the Celt in history. It represents the defeat of the Celtic people by Norseman and Christian alike, and does so with long, vivid reconstructions of primitive consciousness, and with the schematic character counterpointings of romance. The protagonist Aniel, the young druid who must suffer the doubts of a Victorian Hamlet about his place between two worlds, comes to accept the spiritual destiny of his people as a non-historic persistence in joy and serenity, forgotten in defeat, yet the permanent sub-historic ground of all creeds and powers, surviving all. His choices of life and destiny focus on a love triangle - the chief's daughter, amoral and legendary Nessa, who becomes the woman of the triumphant young Viking, and Breeta, the figure of Celtic destiny, earthbound and vital like Mairi of Butcher's Broom. Aniel's suitable choice is Breeta. Gunn's idea of history for the Celt is a rejection of history as a legend having no reality for Celtic destiny.

The Silver Darlings (1941) is quite different; it is Gunn's masterpiece of regional historicity and one of his finest books. The temptation admirably resisted here is to make a period piece, a "romance of the herring industry in the Moray Firth", in the manner of "Paterson's "Behold Thy Daughter" or the Clydeside mercantile romances of Blake. The book includes enough to please such tastes: the rise of prosperous communities on the shores of the Firth, the first shocks to the new prosperity, the plague, the colourful activities of fisherman and curer, the

voyages round Cape Wrath to the Lewis Fishing. But the novel remain
primarily one of more essential and personal dilemmas. Developing
human relations, while illustrative parts of the regional "epic", are fr
of the romance schematism of Sun Circle and the explicit archetypal
forcing of Butcher's Broom.

From Helmsdale, Catrine's husband is carried off by a press gang.
She envisions him dead and walks north to "Dunster" (evidently Dunbeat
scene of Morning Tide, Highland River, Sun Circle), where she lives a
Kirsty Mackay's adopted daughter and heir, and where, in the byre, he
son Finn is born. The young widow-mother's painful growth into her
tragic role is the first narrative centre. Then comes the suitor Roddi
Sinclair, prosperous Dunster fishing captain; and the unfolding world
herring fishing centres on the growth of Finn, his rivalry with Roddie
for his mother, his heroic exploits on Roddie's boat, his achievement
an individual manhood. Narrative setpieces of suspense and excitemer
the fight with the press gang, the stormswept trip around Cape Wrath,
the drunken brawl in Stornaway, Finn's heroic climb up the precipice,
his rescue efforts - abound; yet they alternate with episodes of a fine
and fanciful delicacy in the world of mother and son. Catrine, for all
her tragic role as the bereaved woman, is as profoundly individualized
a female character as any in all Gunn's books. Roddie, the menacing
but heroic fisherman, is as fine a male figure as Gunn has drawn (it is
no accident that the book is dedicated to the memory of his father). Fi
is brought to Hugh and Art, with the additional dimensions of his repre
sentative role in a regional history.

He is no mythic or legendary Finn; his individuality is precious to
him. Yet this individuality depends for its perfection on his becoming
legendary in his own eyes. Through legend the historic self survives,
yet transcends itself, translating its matter of fact into something
"eternally right, like the movement of a figure through the mesh of fat
in one of Hector's old stories, or like a swan on the Irish sea in the
legend of Finn-son-of-Angus." To this other Finn, an old story-teller
on North Uist, he first tells of his fantastic climb up the Flannan preci
pice. It is only as Finn begins his story, as he learns "the power of th
story-teller", that its meaning becomes clear. The old Finn's praise
indicates the thematic importance of storytelling in the novel (and describes Gunn's own ideal of narrative art):

"You told the story well. You brought us into the far deeps of the
sea and we were lost with you in the Beyond where no land is,
only wind and wave and the howling of the darkness. You kept us
in suspense on the cliffs, and you had some art in the way you
referred to our familiars of the other world before you told of

66

the figure of the man you felt by the little stone house. There
you saw no-one and you were anxious to make this clear, smiling at your fancy. It was well enough done. It was all well
done. It was done, too, with the humour that is the play of
drift on the wave. And you were modest. Yet - all that is only
a little - you had something more, my hero, something you will
not know - until you look at it through your eyes, when they are
as old as mine."

By the "power of the story-teller", Finn separates himself from his
mother, reconciles himself to a rival and stepfather, and achieves himself in his own circle. Only the ultimate comic invasion of life itself
can touch him, and in the final chapter the invasion is imminent. Finn,
his manhood achieved, hears love and life coming for him, "the hunters
in the primordial humour . . . closing in"; life, a humorous hunter,
invades his circle. A myth of triumphant and archaic individuality thus
prevails over a novel of regional history.

Finn belongs with Young Art, whose two stories follow his, and who
also triumphs through becoming legendary - but in a very different kind
of book, one which sets the direction for Gunn's later fiction as surely
as The Silver Darlings magnificently recapitulates the earlier novels.

Croft in Houstry Glen

CHECK LIST

1a   <u>The Grey Coast</u>.   London: Cape, 1926.

b   ------------   Boston: Little, Brown, 1926.

c   ------------   Edinburgh: Porpoise Press, 1931.

Reissued after the success of <u>Morning Tide</u>.

2   <u>Hidden Doors</u>. (short stories) Edinburgh: Porpoise Press, 1929
Acknowledgements are made to the editors of "The Dublin
Magazine", "The Scottish Nation", "The Northern Review",
"The Scots Magazine" and "The Cornhill". Seven of the
fifteen stories were reprinted in   <u>The White Hour and other</u>
<u>stories</u>, (1954).

3a   <u>Morning Tide</u>. Edinburgh: Porpoise Press, 1931.
Later impressions give the date of first publication as
January 1931, and this is confirmed by "The English Cata-
logue", but I have found some copies of the first edition in
which the imprint date is 1930. My theory is that publication was planned for late 1930 and printing began with that
imprint date, but that during the course of printing it was
decided to postpone publication to January 1931, and it was
found possible to amend the imprint date while the first
edition was in the press.

b   -----------   Illustrated by Maitland de Gogorza. New York:
Harcourt, Brace, 1931.

c   -----------   London: Faber, 1932. "The Faber Library, 7."

d   -----------   London: Penguin Books, 1936."Penguin Books, 5]

e   -----------   London: Faber, 1953. New edition, reset.

4   <u>Back Home: A play in One Act</u>. Glasgow: W. Wilson, 1932.
"Scottish National Plays Series, 9.
Reprinted in "The Best One-Act Plays of 1931, ed. J. W.
Marriott (London: Harrap, 1932)

The Lost Glen. Edinburgh: Porpoise Press, 1932.

Sun Circle. Edinburgh: Porpoise Press, 1933.

a Butcher's Broom. Edinburgh: Porpoise Press, 1934.

b With title: Highland Night. Illustrated by Freda Bone. New
      York: Harcourt, Brace, 1935.

Whisky and Scotland: A Practical and Spiritual Survey. London:
      Routledge, 1935. "Voice of Scotland" series.

a Highland River. Edinburgh: Porpoise Press, 1937.
      Awarded the James Tait Black Memorial Prize for 1937.

b ------------- Philadelphia: Lippincott, 1937.

c ------------- London: Faber, 1942. New edition, reset.

d ------------- London: Faber, 1943. "'Q' series".

e ------------- Arrow Books, 1960. "Grey Arrow Series".

0 Choosing a Play: A Comedy of Community Drama. Edinburgh:
      Porpoise Press, (1938).
      A reissue of p. 117-40 of "Scottish One-Act Plays", ed.
      John Macnair Reid (Edinburgh: Porpoise Press, 1935).

1 Off in a Boat. London: Faber, 1938.
      Written 'For the crew (his wife), this simple record of
      a holiday in a boat, bought in ignorance and navigated
      by faith and a defective engine'.

2 Old Music. London: Nelson, (1939). "Nelson's Plays for
      Amateurs, 2'. Reprinted in "North Light: Ten New One-Act
      Plays from the North", compiled by Winifred Bannister
      (Glasgow: Maclellan, 1947).

3 Net Results. London: Nelson, (1939). "Nelson's Plays for
      Amateurs, 11".

4 Wild Geese Overhead. London: Faber, 1939.

15 Second Sight. London: Faber, 1940.

16a The Silver Darlings. London: Faber, 1941. Reprinted, London:
Faber, 1969.

b ----------------- New York: G.W. Stewart, 1945.

17a Young Art and Old Hector. London: Faber, 1942.

b ------------- New York: G.W. Stewart, 1944.

18 Storm and Precipice, and Other Pieces. (Selected extracts).
London: Faber, 1942. "Sesame Books".

19a The Serpent. London: Faber, 1943.

b With title: Man Goes Alone. New York: G.W. Stewart, 1944.

c The Serpent. Inverness: Club Leabhar, 1969.

20 The Green Isle of the Great Deep. London: Faber, 1944.

21a The Key of the Chest. London: Faber, 1945.

b --------------- New York: G.W. Stewart, 1946.

22a The Drinking Well. London: Faber, 1946.
Although the imprint date is 1946, it would appear that
publication was delayed until early in 1947. Whitaker
gives the publication date as February 1947, and the
Library of Congress Catalog, more exactly, as February
21, 1947.

b --------------- New York: G.W. Stewart, 1947.

23 The Shadow. London: Faber, 1948.

24 The Silver Bough. London: Faber, 1948.

25 The Lost Chart. London: Faber, 1949.

26   Highland Pack. With drawings by Keith Henderson. London:
        Faber, 1949.
        According to the Foreword, 'most of these notes on country
        life appeared under a pseudonym in the pages of "The Scots
        Magazine" during the early years of the last war'.
        Acknowledgements are also made to the "Glasgow Herald",
        the "S.M.T. (now Scotland's) Magazine" and "Chambers's
        Journal".

27   The White Hour, and Other Stories. London: Faber, 1950.
        'The majority of these stories appeared in the "Scots
        Magazine" over a period of many years; others in
        "Chambers's Journal", the "Cornhill", "Dublin Magazine",
        "Scotland's Magazine", "Scottish Field", "Spectator"; a few
        have been taken from a collection called Hidden Doors
        (1929), now long out of print. Some that might have been
        included are omitted because at least their substance was
        incorporated in novels. Minor revisions have been made.'
        (Author's note). Of the twenty-six stories in this volume
        seven had appeared in Hidden Doors: 'Symbolical', 'Blae-
        berries', 'Such Stuff as Dreams', 'Down to the Sea', 'Half-
        Light', 'The Moor', and the title story, 'The White Hour'.

28   The Well at the World's End. London: Faber, 1951.

29   Bloodhunt. London: Faber, 1952.

30   The Other Landscape. London: Faber, 1954.

31   The Atom of Delight. (Autobiographical) London: Faber, 1956.

(This is a revised form of Dr. Aitken's Check List which appeared as
"Neil Miller Gunn (1891 -), A First Check List of his Books" in "The
Bibliotheck", Volume 3: 1961: Number 3. Thanks are due to the edi-
tor of this periodical for permission to reprint).

TITLES INDEX